PUT THAT LIGHT OUT!

BRITAIN'S CIVIL DEFENCE
SERVICES AT WAR

1939–1945

MIKE BROWN

First published in the United Kingdom in 1999 by
Sutton Publishing Limited · Phoenix Mill
Thrupp · Stroud · Gloucestershire · GL5 2BU

British Library Cataloguing in Publication Data
A catalogue record for this book is available from the British Library

ISBN 0 7509 2210 9

 ALAN SUTTON™ and SUTTON™ are the
trade marks of Sutton Publishing Limited

Typeset in 11/12 pt Ehrhardt.
Typesetting and origination by
Sutton Publishing Limited.
Printed in Great Britain by
Redwood Books

Contents

Acknowledgements

I would like to take this opportunity to thank the following people who so kindly shared their memories with me: Kath Barber, Alan Barron, Mike Bree, Agostino Capaldi, Noel Care, Tim Clarke, Barbara Daltrey, Margaret Ladd (née Cook), Hugh Learmont, Joyce Loysen, Eva Tynan (née Bates), John Wheeler, Len Wright. Also Florrie Padgham for allowing me to use the private memoirs of her husband Frank, and Kath Withersby for those of her brother John (Jack). Thanks also to the following who have kindly loaned photographs: Gus Capaldi (p. 116), Mary Davidson (p. 80), Colin Davis (p. 75), Jimmy Goldsmith (p. 25), George Grigs (p. 96), Margaret Ladd (p. 36), Eva Tynan (p. 113)

Photographs from the following museums, organisations and institutions are reproduced here, with acknowledgement: Imperial War Museum 47, 106, 109; Hull Central Library 2, 6, 12, 15, 30, 38, 43, 70, 79, 110, 115; Kent Messenger Group Newspapers 14, 32, 41, 52, 64, 69, 81, 82, 87, 98, 107; Lewisham Local Studies Centre 8, 11, 16, 22, 24, 33, 34, 39, 40, 49, 55, 59, 60, 67, 76, 78, 111, 114.

Photographs from the contemporary publications listed below have also been used:

Atlas at War 9
Changing Face of Britain 29
Citizens in War – and After 54, 57, 77, 110
Croydon Courageous 62, 71
Croydon and the Second World War 19, 112
Dover Front 83
Fire Service Memories 5, 95

Front Line 51, 97, 118
It Came to Our Door 105
Lloyds under Fire 103
Metropolitan Police at War 17, 85, 86, 87
Ordeal by Fire 7, 18, 26, 61, 99
The Scout (October 1939) 35
The Second Great War 45
Tactical Training in ARP 73

Finally, I should like to thank Jean Wait and John Coulter of Lewisham Local Studies Centre, David Smith of Hull Central Library, Anne Bennett and Jonathan Falconer of Suttons for their help, but most of all Carol, William and Ralph who have had to put up with me.

Every effort has been made to establish and contact copyright holders but this has not been possible in every case. If I have omitted any individuals or organisations I offer my sincere apologies.

Introduction

'Put that light out!' is the one phrase most of us immediately associate with Civil Defence. It conjures up pictures of fire watchers with buckets of sand, and of air raid wardens such as Mr Hodges in *Dad's Army* – figures of fun or, at best, well-meaning amateurs hopelessly attempting to take on the might of Hitler's Luftwaffe. The reality is rather different.

True, they *were* mostly amateurs, but civil defence was far more than just a few wardens trying to maintain the blackout; it was a whole series of services designed to counter every effect of an aerial assault, co-ordinated centrally by the local authority. As for figures of fun, 2,379 civil defence workers were killed in the line of duty and 4,459 seriously injured. Eva Tynan, who served in the fire service in London during the blitz said recently: 'I get angry: we had Remembrance Sunday last month and no one from the fire service was allowed to march past the Cenotaph. I get an extra sixpence a week on my pension, and I didn't even get my [defence] medal.'

As the years have passed public perception of the bombing has focused on London, which did indeed receive by far the most attacks, but other cities, towns, and villages throughout the UK, including Northern Ireland, were attacked. Some, like Coventry and Plymouth, suffered far more in relation to their size than anything that the capital as a whole experienced. Most people born after the war know that bombing took place, but few are aware of its scale; to hear London firemen tell of an almost unbroken chain of warehouses ablaze along the Thames from the Tower of London to Deptford evokes a scene beyond the imagination of most of us: to hear of the 'big blitz' when London was bombed virtually every night for three months beggars belief.

One of the reasons for this lack of knowledge is the success of British propaganda at the time. Indeed it was so successful that one person I interviewed told me: 'We didn't have propaganda – that was the Germans!' The censors allowed very little information on the raids to be reported, and few, if any, details of Civil Defence activity. There was a spate of local publications soon after the war with titles such as *Trial by Ordeal – Malden faces Total War* and *Croydon Courageous*, but by then the euphoria of victory had passed and the reality of austerity Britain had sunk in, so such books rarely sold well. Thus the work of the Civil Defence Services, and the heroism shown by so many of their members, was almost forgotten. This book is a small attempt to remember them, and their work.

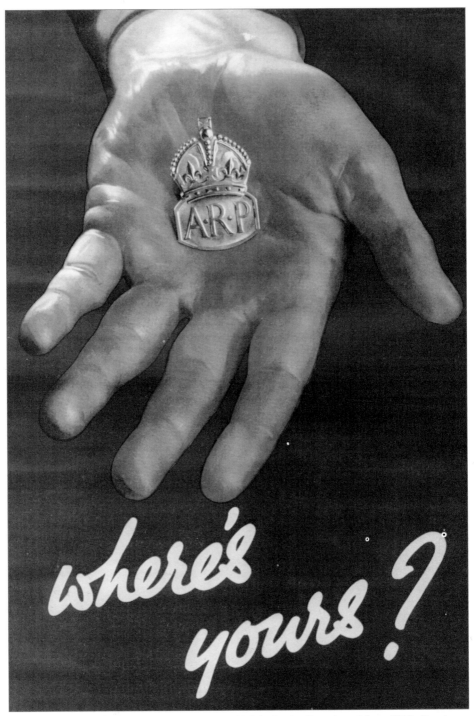

Early ARP recruiting poster. The badge is the ARP badge in silver, issued from 1937. For three years, along with an armband and helmet, it remained the only uniform for most ARP workers.

CHAPTER 1

The Build-up to War

The term 'Civil Defence' began to be used in the late 1930s to cover a group of services whose task was either wholly or mainly to counter the growing threat of air raids. This task might be to minimise bombing casualties by taking measures before the raid, such as providing gas masks, or to deal with the injuries and destruction caused by the raids, by organisations such as the casualty services.

Air raids on Britain had first taken place during the First World War; the first bomb was dropped near Dover Castle by a solitary German aircraft in December 1914. During the following year, Britain experienced nineteen raids by German Zeppelins, massive air-ships, and on 31 May London was bombed for the first time. These Zeppelin raids continued until January 1916, by which time British defences, including searchlights and anti-aircraft guns, had made raids by slow-moving airships far too expensive in men and machines.

The war led to tremendous developments in aircraft and bomb technology and raiding began again in May 1917, this time by twin-engined Gotha heavy bombers. London experienced its worst raid one month later when 162 civilians were killed. By this time rumours were rife that the horror weapon of the trenches, gas, was to be dropped in the raids – but it never was.

Over the course of the war, about 1,400 civilians were killed in just over 100 raids. Many of the responsive measures utilised in the Second World War such as air raid warnings, shelters, gas masks, searchlights and anti-aircraft guns, were originally used in the First World War but the raiding was on a comparatively small scale and the aftermath of damage, fire and injury could be dealt with by the existing emergency services, with some help from the army.

In the interwar years, aviation development continued with ever larger aircraft able to fly faster, further and with larger payloads. In Britain, with another war becoming a serious possibility, the Committee for Imperial Defence set up a subcommittee whose function was to look at 'the organisation for war, including Civil Defence, home defence, censorship and war emergency legislation'. This group was to be called the Air Raid Precautions (or ARP) subcommittee; it met for the first time in May 1924 with Sir John Anderson in the chair. Among the topics discussed by the group were warnings, prevention of damage including lighting restrictions, shelters, gas-masks and evacuation, and repair of damage, including the medical care of casualties. For the next nine years the subcommittee carried out its work in classic Whitehall secrecy.

King and queen with warden 'whitehats', Hull, August 1941. Note the early diamond rank markings on the three rear wardens' helmets, one diamond signifying a head warden, and two a divisional warden, who is also wearing a Civil Defence armband. (Hull Central Library)

In March 1933 the subcommittee looked at who should be in charge of Britain's ARP services; they decided that local authorities would be the most suitable agency. Later a circular was sent to all local authorities outlining the proposed ARP scheme; it included details about forming first aid, anti-gas and rescue parties. A new department of the Home Office, the ARP Department, was formed in 1935 under the control of Wing Commander E.J. Hodsall, later Sir John Hodsall, who had been secretary to the ARP subcommittee since 1929.

In March 1935 Hitler announced to the world that Germany, in direct contra-vention of the Versailles Treaty, had re-established her air force and introduced military conscription. The ARP Department immediately set to work, issuing a circular in July which set out in some detail 'the precautionary measures necessary for safeguarding the civil population against the effects of any possible attack by hostile aircraft'. From the beginning the department began to issue handbooks on subjects such as: 'Anti-gas precautions and first aid for air raid casualties', 'Anti-gas precautions for merchant shipping', and 'Incendiary bombs and fire precautions'.

At first ARP was widely considered as a joke: indeed much of the makeshift nature of the early services only seemed to encourage such a view, as would its formation date – 1 April.

In July 1936, civil war erupted in Spain. It began as a series of risings by right-wing elements in the Spanish military against the left-wing government of the Republic. Soon the conflict began to represent the clash of ideologies, left and right, and volunteers flocked from all over Europe and beyond. The fascist governments of Germany and Italy sent 'volunteers' and materials, including aircraft. The civil war became a testing ground for bombing tactics, including attacks on Madrid, and more infamously, Guernica. Graphic cinema newsreel footage of the aftermath of the raids, including the mangled bodies of women and children, served to create public concern in Britain. Mike Bree, from Penzance, remembered:

> the cinema newsreels that showed footage of that attack and its aftermath. In particular I always recall a large, front-page, newspaper picture showing a mother, dishevelled and blood-spattered, sitting in the street with shattered buildings just behind her head, holding up her tear-stained face towards the cameraman. She had her mouth open, crying; her hand is raised as though for help; across her soiled lap lies the tiny body of her young child, clothes tattered and disarrayed, some wounds evident. I'm quite sure that particular shot brought home to all who saw it the realisation: 'My God, this could be my street, my family, any time' – it did me!

In January 1937, the first official radio broadcast on ARP matters described some of the government's plans and appealed for volunteers for the ARP services. Local progress in setting up these services varied enormously; in some areas, large-scale exercises took place, some of which included the new ARP Wardens' Service. In other areas, ARP had yet to leave the drawing board.

At this point, uniform was not provided. Wardens wore only a silver ARP badge and a helmet, usually marked with a letter/letters denoting the wearer's service. Often there was also some indication of rank on the helmet, such as stripes or diamonds; commonly, officers' helmets were painted white, earning them the nickname of whitehats. It was quite a common practice to issue personnel with armbands which, like the helmet, were marked with the service of the wearer, but some also showed the rank and/or local authority.

A great deal of the ARP preparations were based on the experience of Spain. An ARP Department inspector spent some time there in late 1937, studying the effects of German and Italian bombing and evaluating the defensive measures employed. Based on this, it was projected that 120,000 British civilians would be killed in the first week of a future war, with about twice that number injured. For many people this increased the view that Britain should avoid a European conflict at any cost, adding to the popularity of appeasement. ARP measures were often seen as militaristic and provocative. A letter dated July 1938 to the *Lewisham Borough News* from the Propaganda Secretary of the Lewisham branch of the Peace Pledge Union stated: 'As people entered the hall, they were handed a leaflet "Preparing for Peace" which asserted the folly of armaments, including ARP, pointing out that this country had broken her pledge to disarm by consistently re-arming since the Great War. The inadequacy and false security of ARP were dealt with, together with the facts that ARP are part of the war machine and make right international relations increasingly difficult.'

On the first day of 1938, the ARP Act came into force. This compelled local authorities to set up ARP schemes and gave an outline of such schemes. It required the local authorities to set up wardens, first aid, emergency ambulance, gas decontamination, rescue, repair and demolition services, as well as setting up first aid posts, gas cleansing stations and casualty clearing stations. They were also obliged to expand the local fire services by forming and equipping an Auxiliary Fire Service.

The Act settled one of the main obstacles to the setting up of local schemes – the ever-present question of money. County councils and boroughs were asked to submit plans which, if approved, became eligible for government grants of from 60 to 75 per cent of the cost of the scheme. Many authorities which had refused to start any ARP work until financial responsibility was clarified now began to push ahead, although there continued to be a vast difference in the response by different local authorities.

Sir Warren Fisher had been asked to look into the control of ARP and in 1938 he proposed that, in the event of war, a new minister, the Minister of Home

---

In *It Came to Our Door*, H.P. Twyford recalled: 'Some months before war broke out, I was assigned by the *Western Morning News* to visit every town, large and small, in the West-country and report on their preparedness to meet enemy air attack. There was no censorship in those days, and one could write freely. I found an amazing divergence of opinion and readiness. In some places there were public men who flatly pooh-poohed the idea of air raid precautions being necessary.

"We are too far away".

"A sheer waste of public money."

Those were some of the remarks I heard. In most places, however, there was some measure of doubt and fear in the minds. "Better be prepared", they said. So it was that while some set about their preparations wholeheartedly, others did so with less enthusiasm and in a few places, there was a contented policy of drift.'

Women's Auxiliary Fire Service parade being inspected by Commander Firebrace on Clapham Common, October 1938.

Defence, be appointed to have direct control of Civil Defence. Fisher also recommended the development of a regional organisation. Both proposals were accepted, and the country was divided into twelve regions, ten in England and one each in Scotland and Wales, and for each of the regions a regional commissioner was appointed. It is interesting that the regions controlled by these commissioners were almost exactly the same as those controlled by Oliver Cromwell's inspectors general.

In March the Home Secretary made a second radio appeal for a million volunteers; this reflected the prevailing apathy towards Civil Defence matters. He made a point of the need for men and women to train as wardens. Then, in September, the general public's view was changed dramatically. Hitler demanded that part of Czechoslovakia bordering Germany, called the Sudetenland, be given to Germany. His argument was that the Sudetenland contained many people of German descent who were suffering discrimination. Czechoslovakia refused to give way; suddenly a European war seemed inevitable. In Britain trenches were dug in public parks, the ARP services were put on standby, and press reports became ever gloomier. Prime Minister Neville Chamberlain flew to meet Hitler

Recruiting drive for rescue service, Hull. (Hull Central Library)

for one last effort. Then it was announced that Chamberlain had achieved 'peace for our time' in Munich. Italy, France, and Britain gave away the Sudetenland to Germany, giving Czechoslovakia no say.

The Munich Crisis was at first followed by a wave of relief, but this soon gave way to deep apprehension. Hitler's first 'territorial demands' in the Saar, the Rhineland and Austria, had been seen as putting right the unfair conditions of the Versailles Treaty. These places had, after all, historically all been part of a greater, German-speaking whole. This could not be argued in the case of the Sudetenland, where German moves could be seen as nothing other than aggressive expansionism. Peace may have been bought, but from now on few in Britain had any illusions about Hitler. Many people now believed that the question of another war was 'when', rather than 'if'.

ARP began to be taken increasingly seriously. Where before local papers had rarely referred to it, in most, hardly a week went by without some mention of the subject. The appointment of local officers, public meetings, training exercises, recruitment drives, and the numbers coming forward for training rose dramatically. In the immediate aftermath, the *Daily Herald* of 1 October 1938 reported that '. . . the drive for ARP recruits goes on', and an official of the Home Office told the *Herald* that 'thousands more are still wanted. "Winter lectures on ARP will be intensive. And we expect the volunteers to roll up again."'

The great majority of ARP workers were to be part-time, unpaid volunteers; they were expected to work for a maximum of 48 hours each month, although most of them worked considerably longer than this. In February 1939 it was announced in parliament that full-time ARP personnel were to be paid: £3 a week for men, £2 for women. Skilled rescue workers were paid more, in line with construction industry rates. Later in the year, pay for part-time members was agreed for time spent on air raid call-out.

That year the planning and implementation of local ARP schemes moved forward at great speed, while the situation in Europe continued to worsen. During the year a series of trial blackouts took place, during which all the Civil Defence services, including the fire-fighting forces and the police, carried out operations dealing with imaginary incidents. In spite of all the preparations which had gone before, it still came as a shock to many to see volunteers lying in the streets, often luridly made up, to represent the dead and injured. In July, the Civil Defence Act was passed, putting ARP on a statutory basis.

On 1 September Germany invaded Poland. From that date, blackout restrictions were imposed in Britain and the Auxiliary Fire Service mobilised.

London's AFS officers, September 1939, left to right: Col A.C.H. Maclean, F.W. Jackson (Dept Chief Officer LFB), Mrs J. Roster, Commander A.N.G. Firebrace (Chief Officer LFB), C.M. Giveen (Senior Deputy Commandant AFS), T.H. Hutchinson.

Over the next two days, local ARP schemes came into operation: first aid posts, rescue, decontamination and ambulance depots, and wardens' posts started to function, and were staffed full-time.

George Grigs, an auxiliary fireman, recalls, 'As the certainty of war became imminent we non-regulars were working on the basis of 48 hours on duty and 24 hours off. I had a flat in the Earls Court area at the time, and was relaxing after a bath on that fateful morning when Chamberlain announced that "this country is a war with Germany".

Hastily donning my uniform I rushed out to try to get a taxi to take me to my unit, but by that time the air raid warning (a false alarm, as it transpired) had sounded, and it took me a while to find a driver prepared to accept me as a fare. All I can remember about the journey was the deserted and quiet streets – and an abandoned car in the otherwise empty open spaces of Hyde Park Corner.'

Early stretcher party depot. Notice the almost complete lack of uniform, and the range of 'ARP Mobile Units'. (Lewisham Local Studies)

CHAPTER 2

The ARP Services in Wartime

As soon as it became clear that war was inevitable, preparations went into over-drive. Premises suitable for conversion to posts and depots were found, personnel placed on a full-time basis, recruitment drives initiated and training pushed forward. According to the civil defence records of the City of Gloucester, 'Training during that first winter was difficult. Based mostly on theory, much of it had to be evolved at Posts and Depots. Instructors and equipment were at a premium. But thanks to the enthusiasm and energy of the pioneers, training went on and the various Departments of ARP gradually prepared themselves for action.'

This was new ground, for the experience of bombing in the First World War was on such a small scale compared with what was expected that it was of little or no use. Certainly lessons were learnt in Spain which helped to shape the ARP services, but by far the greater part of the organisation had to be worked out as they went, and changes made as faults in the system became apparent. But this was not all: the development of civil defence became a chess game between the defenders and the Luftwaffe. Each ARP development was followed by new weapons, some of them aimed directly at the CD services. So the organisation had to be in a continual state of development, as each new lesson was learned.

One of the early lessons concerned air raid warnings; the aim of the warning system was to give five minutes' warning of approaching enemy aircraft. This meant dividing the country into

Roof watchers on top of the Atlas building in London during the V-weapon assault later in the war. The woman is wearing the civilian-style helmet.

100 warning districts to interfere as little as possible with everyday activities. However, over the course of 1940 the incidence of warnings increased rapidly, usually with no ensuing raid. For the general public this was irritating, but for the hard-pressed war factories each false alarm was as bad as a real raid as workers filed into their shelters and vital production was lost. So serious was this loss of production that Germany introduced 'nuisance raiders', usually single aircraft which would, to use the RAF expression, 'stooge around', leaving a series of areas under warning in their wake. In September of that year the Ministry of Home Security introduced the idea of the 'Industrial Warning System'. By this system the public siren was regarded only as an alert; each factory in the system would deploy 'roof spotters', who would sound an alarm only if enemy aircraft were seen approaching. The system proved so effective that workers were in the shelters when the factories were attacked, even when the sirens had failed to warn civilians in the area.

Other developments were to cut down on the time the siren was sounded, as the sound itself had a bad effect on morale, and to improve the warnings given to the CD services. The public were only aware of the sirens, but the CD services had a series of telephone warnings based on colours: for example, preliminary warning yellow was passed on to control about ten minutes before the siren was sounded. This indicated that enemy raiders were headed in their general direction and allowed the various Civil Defence depots and posts to be put in readiness, although often no attack would develop in that area. The siren would not be sounded until action warning red.

Attracting sufficient volunteers had always been a problem, and although this improved after Munich there was still a shortfall. At the beginning of the war the Defence (General) Regulations empowered the Home Secretary to conscript people into fire watching or part-time ARP work. When the expected hordes of bombers failed to materialise in these early stages, there were calls to cut down the numbers of civil defenders. 'It was stated at a meeting of Croydon Town Council that there were a lot of cases where husbands had good jobs and their wives were taking ARP jobs for pin money', the *Evening Standard* reported on 26 September 1939. Two weeks later, on 4 October, the *Standard* reported that 'The Mayor of Gillingham told members of the town council that he had found ARP wardens asleep at their posts'. He had made unannounced visits. 'The Rev. J.D. Jones said that five wardens stationed near his vicarage appeared to be playing darts most of the time.' There was some official cutting back, but numbers fell far more sharply as volunteers left, through boredom or disillusionment, or as a result of continual jibes from the press, the public and the politicians.

The air assault on Britain went through several stages: the first phase, up to May 1940, had mainly taken the form of bomb attacks, or minelaying, by single or small groups of aircraft, against ships or coastal towns, mirroring the Phoney War. (While it was phoney for most, the Merchant Navy was in the middle of a genuine struggle.) In the second phase the assault moved mainly to the ports, manufacturing areas and airfields of the south-east, although there were several night attacks further afield, especially on the Midlands and Merseyside. This was the period of Blitzkrieg in Europe, and Britain was being softened up for a German invasion of the south coast.

Fire guards being trained by wardens, October 1941. Both the wardens (right, and left wearing helmet) are wearing the earliest bluette overall uniform, with chrome ARP buttons. The warden on the right is a post warden, shown by the early red bar-and-diamond rank marking on his cuff. (Lewisham Local Studies)

Following the Luftwaffe's failure to defeat the RAF, the next phase was an attempt to break down the morale of the British public. On Saturday 7 September wave after wave of German bombers followed the line of the Thames and struck east London, concentrating on the docks. The raid continued until early next morning. Casualties were high: over 400 dead, and Black Saturday, as it became known, marked the start of the big blitz (sometimes called the Battle of London). Next night, the bombers returned, as they did almost every night for the next three months.

Also during September, the Luftwaffe began to drop land mines, or parachute mines. These were actually magnetic sea-mines, but the Royal Navy's measures against them had become so effective that their use at sea diminished considerably. Consequently they were used against land targets – and were a formidable weapon. In *It Came to Our Door*, H.P. Twyford gives a striking example of their power: 'I well remember what I think must have been about the first of these land mines which fell in the city. It was late one evening, and I was standing outside the Mount Gold First Aid Post in Edith Avenue when the raid took place. We actually saw the mine dropping by parachute. It fell in open ground adjoining some allotments at Prince Rock – the best part of a mile away. The blast came to us like the lash of a whip. There were no serious casualties, but the blast ripped the roofs and blew out the windows and doors of hundreds of houses in the vicinity.'

On 4 October Sir John Anderson became Lord President of the Council, being replaced as Minister of Home Security by Herbert Morrison, ex-leader of London County Council. Many welcomed the move. Under Sir John the ministry had refused the calls for deep shelters, and no-one had made much provision for those left homeless. Black Saturday had graphically shown the need for both. In its report that day, the *Daily Mirror* said: 'Sir John Anderson has haply (*sic*) received a more decorative and less responsible post.'

Returning to May 1940, the success of the Blitzkrieg in Europe and the fear of an invasion of England led to the formation of the Local Defence Volunteers, later called the Home Guard, which drew off thousands of potential volunteers. This, the need for factory workers and the ever-increasing calls of the services, severely strained the CD services. By the beginning of 1941 things had deteriorated to the extent that the Minister of Home Security had to issue the first Civil Defence Compulsory Enrolment Order, which stated that all males between sixteen and sixty not already doing Civil Defence or Home Guard service must do up to 48 hours fire watching a month.

At first, it was felt that uniform should not be worn by ARP workers, to emphasise their civilian status. However some local authorities, recognising the positive effect that a uniform could have on the solidarity and morale of the service,

Visit to Hull by the Minister of Health, Ernest Brown, June 1941. The two women flanking him are wearing ARP felt hats, as is the woman second from the right, although she is still wearing her badge on her lapel. The three women on the left are in first pattern bluette raincoats, which, as can clearly be seen, did not fit very well. (Hull Central Library)

began to provide some of their personnel with a kind of uniform, usually boiler suits or overalls, although most continued to rely on armbands or lettered helmets. Authorities became concerned that volunteers were using the expensive anti-gas protection suits to cover their own clothes while on duty, so in July 1939 the Home Secretary told parliament that the government would provide local authorities with grants to supply their ARP personnel with free uniforms. It was not until October that authorities were told that supplies of uniforms would shortly be available. These early uniforms were overalls for men, and Macintosh-type overall coats for women, both in dark blue 'bluette', a type of denim. These were useful for protecting the wearer's clothes, but were not particularly weatherproof, especially against the cold. It was at this time that many of the more confusing local variations began to appear.

On 14 November 1940 a similar-sized attack to that of Black Saturday hit Coventry. Casualties were on a similar scale, but the attack was concentrated on the centre of a much smaller town, destroying almost one-third of the houses. Administrative centres, shops, food stores and vital services – gas, water, electricity – were all destroyed. Vaccination centres were set up to inoculate against typhoid, and food supplies had to be rushed in as most of the rest centres had been put out of action. Coventry Cathedral, reduced to a shell, became the symbol of the town's suffering, and the Germans coined a new word, to 'Coventrate' – to destroy the very heart of a town by massed, concentrated bombing.

On the night of 29 December it was the City of London's turn to be Coventrated. A massive incendiary raid took place on the City, causing such devastation that it soon came to be known as 'The Second Great Fire of London'. Few fire watchers were on duty, this being a weekend in the holiday season, so the fires ran unchecked. This was the evening when St Paul's Cathedral was ringed by fire, and photographs of that scene are still some of the most memorable of the war. The event caused the government to rethink its approach to fire fighting and led to the creation of the Fire Guard. For the next five months, the cities of Britain, including Plymouth, Manchester, Portsmouth and Merseyside, experienced similar concentrated raids.

Towards the end of the year the Germans made another move in the chess game with Britain's civil defenders. Among the different kinds of incendiaries they now began to drop explosive ones. These looked just like the others, but carried just enough of an explosive charge to kill or disable anyone too near. It was a device aimed specifically at members of Civil Defence.

The danger did not come from bombs alone, as this report from the *Sussex Express and County Herald* shows: 'It was only a few seconds before these bombs were dropped that Mr W.P. Tomley, who had done so much for the town in terms of ARP matters, lost his life. . . . Within a few seconds of the plane being heard, Mr Tomley was on his way to the Control Room at Crouch House. He had just got to the junction of Vicarage Walk and Warwick Road when he ran into the line of fire of the German machine gunners, and received a bullet wound in the chest, from which he died immediately.' In 1943 it was announced that a grant of up to £7 10s might be made towards the private funeral of a Civil Defence volunteer killed in the line of duty.

From February 1941 a heavy battledress uniform was issued, first to rescue parties, then to the other services. Thus evolved the full uniform of blouse,

Maidstone CD personnel doing rifle training with Home Guard instructors, January 1942. Some of the trainees are wearing Home Guard armbands with their CD uniforms. (Kent Messenger Group Newspapers)

trousers, greatcoat and beret, with the options of skirt, ski cap or felt hat for the female volunteers. Some personnel – emergency mortuary service operatives, for instance – were never issued with a uniform. Instead they received a Civil Defence armband bearing the words CIVIL DEFENCE in an arc, flanked with curved lines and surmounted with a crown.

In May 1941 a circular set out the duties of the local authorities in the event of an invasion, including setting up a Defence Committee. Members of this committee included the ARP controller and the chief officers of the police and fire services. In some areas, large numbers of the CD services were trained in the use of arms, members of first aid parties were to become Home Guard medical orderlies, and wardens were expected to lead the public, to advise them to remain where they were and to stay with them to continue with the work of Civil Defence.

During 1941, the phrase ARP started to be phased out in favour of Civil Defence, to 'emphasise the growth and increased importance of what were known originally as the ARP General Services and their essential unity with other branches of civil defence' (ARP Training Bulletin no. 7). From this point the names of the services changed: for instance, the Rescue Service became the Civil Defence Rescue Service. The names ARP controller and ARP officer were kept, reflecting the fact that neither controlled nor was in charge of the police and the fire service, the other branches of Civil Defence. The other main change was the replacement of the red ARP breast badge with a yellow CD one.

Depot officers with head of service. This clearly shows the second pattern uniform for men. The head of service, centre, is in plain clothes but is wearing the ARP instructor's lapel badge; this was normal for heads of service. (Hull Central Library)

'Uncle Will and Margaret'. The caption tells us that Margaret and the much-bemedalled Uncle Will are in Maesteg. Margaret is looking very smart in her obviously new uniform – the badge is still stiff, and you can see where the sleeves have been let down. The ski-cap and trousers suggest the ambulance service.

The big blitz on Britain finally came to an end in June 1941, when Germany switched its attention to the attack on Russia on the 22nd. Raiding was cut back drastically, and the next six months, though certainly not raid-free, were, nevertheless, something of a respite.

In July the next phase began, the tip and run raids – fast, low-level, daylight attacks by single or small groups of fighter-bombers. The damage caused was often quite different from that resulting from a high-level raid. Bombs released from a great height strike more or less vertically, so that buildings are damaged from the top downward. But these bombs were dropped at low level and so travelled horizontally, where they were more likely to hit a wall than the roof. This often resulted in the greatest damage being done to the lower floors, leaving upper levels hanging precariously above, adding to the danger to both those trapped and to the rescuers. Furthermore, there were more likely to be casualties surviving in the upper levels, and systems had to be devised to lower them down from above. Noel Care, first aid party member, recalled: 'There was one horrific hit and run raid.

Rescue men lower stretcher from window, August 1941. (Lewisham Local Studies)

Eighteen bombs fell in 30 seconds, one hit a couple of houses in the old town, another hit the wing of a hotel. It went in through a window, through the room and came out the other side, hit the centre wing and went off. Unfortunately it was full of Canadian troops.' These tip and run raids continued until January 1944.

In August 1941 the Fire Guard were formed, and at the same time the multitude of small brigades which formed Britain's fire services were amalgamated into the National Fire Service. This was Britain's counter to the fire bomb menace.

The Baedeker raids, otherwise known as spite raids, began with a raid on Bath on 25 April 1942. These attacks, on Britain's historic cathedral towns and cities such as York, Exeter, Canterbury and Norwich, continued until July. They were the Luftwaffe's revenge for the RAF's raid on the ancient German cities of Rostock and Lübeck, vital Baltic supply ports and aircraft and ship-building centres, and got their name from the famous Baedeker travel guides, which, it was said at the time, the Germans used to choose their targets.

Kath Barber drove an ARP ambulance in Exeter during the raid of 24 May 1942: 'You know, Exeter was one of the cities which had spite raids. I was on night duty and drove safely through that early morning without injury – it was terrible. . . . Two messenger boys attached to No. 4 Post carried on delivering messages to the Wardens' Post through the night on foot after their bikes were blown from under them.' In January 1943, as a result of manpower shortages, the first aid parties were merged into the light rescue service.

Policemen, firemen and ARP workers engaged in rescue work. That this is not an exercise is obvious from their grave expressions – in fact this is Sandhurst Road School, Catford, in January 1943. A single tip and run raider dropped a 500 kg bomb on the school at lunchtime – when these rescuers dug out the dead and injured the death toll was 38 children and 6 teachers.

Between January and March 1944 there were a series of raids which came to be known as the little blitz. One of its features was the dropping of large numbers of incendiary bombs on fairly small areas, with the aim of swamping local fire guards. The little blitz was carried out using the tactic which had come to be called 'scalded cat raids' – short, sharp, high-level raids by fast aircraft.

On 13 June 1944 the first V-1 flying bomb fell in Bethnal Green, and on 8 September the first V-2 rocket landed in Chiswick. The V-weapon attack, the last

The next morning. Firemen in waterproofs are still at work the day after a raid.

phase of the assault, carried on until 28 March 1945. It was among the worst assaults of the entire war. In Croydon, for instance, the worst hit of the London boroughs, the official figures for flying bomb damage was 211 killed and 1,991 injured; 1,400 houses destroyed and 54,000 damaged. This was caused by a total of 141 bombs.

Eva Tynan, a London firewoman, said: 'Later, the doodlebugs wiped whole streets out – there was nothing left – that was it. There were five streets blasted off the Old Kent Road; one poor man came along, he was looking for his wife. He found her hand with the rings still on it – she'd been blown to bits. I served right through to the end of the war. It was an awful time – I was glad when it was all over.'

In spite of this, civil defence numbers began to be cut back from September 1944. Mike Bree, First Aid Party member, remembers: 'The "wind-down" of Civil Defence came, for me, with the close of 1944 with the easing of the much hated blackout. We did not suddenly see "the lights go on again" or "get lit up when the lights go up in London", as we had sung, and dreamed of, for so long. First we had the "dim-out" – a partial blackout which came in September 1944. The blackout regulations were relaxed inland, but not within a coastal strip extending five miles in from the sea, all round our shores. For Christmas Day 1944, inland churches were allowed to light up their stained glass windows, and just after that, car headlights could have their slit-masks removed. From that point onwards many of the more petty restrictions were lifted, but we, on the coast, went on as before.'

At the end of April 1945 it was announced that all the Civil Defence General Services would be wound up on 2 May. The CD services held a final parade on 10 June in Hyde Park, reviewed by the king. As only one representative from each district was allowed to attend, many local parades also took place.

CHAPTER 3
Structure and Organisation

Defence against air raids was split into two parts. The first of these was active defence, made up of fighter aircraft, searchlights, anti-aircraft guns, barrage balloons and radar; these were all operated by the military. The second was at first called passive defence and was in three sections:

1   The police, including war reserve police, special constables (which included the Observer Corps until 1939), and the women's auxiliary police.
2   The fire brigades, including the Auxiliary Fire Service and the Women's Auxiliary Fire Service.
3   The ARP services, later known as the Civil Defence general services. These included the Report and Control, messenger and wardens' services, the engineer services comprising rescue, repair and demolition (combined or separate), the anti-gas services; decontamination and gas identification, and

Croydon: flying bomb incident, Upper Norwood, June 1944. The Morrison shelter is battered, but still in one piece. Note the widespread damage caused by the bomb, and the council engineer's helmet marking – E.

the casualty services, which included first aid parties, first aid posts, emergency ambulances, stretcher parties and the emergency mortuary service. The WVS was founded as a support service in 1938, and in 1941 the Fire Guard organisation was set up.

The functions of passive defence were fivefold: (a) air raid warnings; (b) prevention of damage. This included gas masks, air raid shelters and the blackout; (c) the repair of damage; (d) the maintenance of essential services; (e) informing the public about the dangers of air attack and the various precautionary measures. This was done by house-to-house visits, leaflets, posters, and public meetings.

Local authority control of ARP dictated the nature of the fledgling general services. Instead of the quasi-military ethos that might have been fostered in a national body, the service evolved into groups of volunteer civilians under the control of local dignitaries or civil servants. This was reflected in the fact that there was to be no uniform or ranks, no saluting or military-style discipline. This is clearly shown in this report from the *Lewisham Borough News* of 6 August 1941:

ARP MAN NEGLECTS HIS DUTY

Mr CB of Forest Hill, a driver in the Lewisham Rescue Party Service, was summoned at Greenwich police court, on July 30, for absenting himself from duty at the North Lewisham depot without authority. The officer in charge of the depot said that at two o'clock in the morning of June 23 an air raid was in progress – he ordered a roll call, and found CB was missing. A thorough search was made of all places, including lorries, where he might be hiding, but nothing was seen of him until 7.45 a.m., when he (CB) reported to him and said he had been hiding in a dustcart. Witness mentioned that last November a bomb struck the depot, killing one man and injuring many, including the defendant, who was taken to hospital.

CB said the bomb last November burst nine feet away and blew him on top of two men. He received injuries to his eyes, his head and ears, and was still receiving hospital treatment as an outpatient. As a result of his experience he went cold when the siren sounded, and in a raid his 'head splits and his brain seems to turn over'. Nevertheless, he had been out on scores of raids . . . When the siren went on June 23 he 'came over queer' and went to a dustcart. He mentioned, incidentally, that he assisted in the invention of a safety chair to rescue casualties from upper windows. The Magistrate fined him 40s.

Had he been in the services, this would have been a serious court martial offence, instead he was fined by the local bench.

Although there were to be no ranks as such, it was clear that a chain of command was necessary, especially in the case of large-scale bomb damage, or 'incidents' as they were known, where many different individuals and services were involved. Thus small groups such as stretcher parties were to have leaders. Another important point is that by far the biggest part of the general services were volunteers, so that the response to a typical sergeant-major-type 'request', might well have been, 'blow this, I'm off!', or words to that effect. In the rescue service training manual this is summed up as follows: 'It is the Leader's duty to ensure that the instructions and wishes of his superior officer are faithfully carried out by himself and his men . . . to foster the loyalty of his men, both to himself and to those in authority; to earn their confidence in him and his ability . . . The Leader can best do this by encouragement and by example, by teaching his men to co-operate as a team and carry out their duties in a spirit of keenness and willingness. To win the confidence of his team, the Leader must be quite clear in his mind as to what he wants done, how he wants it done, and the reason why it is to be done at all. He should take an impartial interest in each of his men, try to realise their possibilities, and be watchful for their welfare in the widest sense.'

One advantage to local control was that the structure of local civil defence organisations reflected the needs of, and potential threats to, the local community, be it a small county town, city, port or village. Thus each local ARP organisation was different, with variations in structure, numbers, functions and, after their introduction, ranks, uniforms and badges. One example of this arose after the creation in 1940 of the Home Guard. In some areas, ARP personnel were actively encouraged to be members of the Home Guard, while in other places such as London it was discouraged, or even forbidden.

The following imaginary incident gives a picture of the parts played by the various ARP general services: a high explosive bomb has fallen on 97 Nonsuch Avenue. Hearing the explosion, a pair of local wardens hurries to the scene. There they take stock of the situation, and one hurries back to their post, where a report on the incident is sent by telephone or messenger to the authority's Report and Control Centre. There, the local ARP controller decides, on the basis of the information received, which services are required; in this case the report states that a fire has broken out and that a family of four live in the house, who usually shelter under the stairs. The building has largely collapsed and there is no sign of the occupants. He therefore contacts the fire service control room, the rescue service, first aid party and emergency ambulance depots. These in turn send out the squads they feel necessary to do the job.

Back at the incident, the remaining warden, waiting to direct the services to the bombed building, is rejoined by her partner returning from the post. On arrival, the rescue party and other services are briefed on the situation by the wardens, at which point the party leader may decide to contact their depot superintendent for reinforcements, special equipment, etc. The wardens take charge of co-ordinating the work of the other parties until a senior officer arrives. In the case of a large incident, a specially trained incident officer, usually a warden or a policeman, is sent to take over. The firemen fight the fire and the rescue party locate and release the trapped family. Then the first aid party decides whether their injuries can be treated on the spot or whether to send the family, via the emergency ambulance service, to a first aid post or, in the case of serious injury, to a casualty clearing hospital. As the incident is brought under control, the various services return to their depots.

CHAPTER 4
Training

Training was at the heart of civil defence. A new service, with new procedures, it could only work if all its members were trained to a high degree of readiness, and throughout the organisation great stress was laid on training and exercises. The ARP Act of 1938 gave local authorities the duty of training ARP personnel, and the ARP training plan was initiated by the Inspector General and his staff. This department continued throughout the war to lay down the principles of training, which for most was organised in three stages.

STAGE 1   Basic training. This was common to all ARP services and consisted of understanding the organisation of ARP, dealing with incendiaries and HE (high explosive) bombs, anti-gas measures, and first aid.

Wardens' training. Some areas included army-style obstacle courses in their training schemes for ARP workers. Of interest here is the non-regulation windcheater worn by the trainer on the right: in the early days many local, or personal, variations in uniforms appeared. Despite the ARP and local area badges, this appears to be a completely personal creation. (Lewisham Local Studies)

STAGE 2   Service training. This consisted of specialist training peculiar to each particular service, with great emphasis on team training.

STAGE 3   Inter-service training. This consisted of training in parties or squads with groups from other services, usually on realistic exercises, in order that each service should know how the others operated, and learn how to work together.

All three stages were carried out locally by instructors, supported by a plethora of training manuals, handbooks, memoranda and pamphlets issued by the ministry, the local authorities and commercial publishers.

One part of anti-gas training was a visit to the gas van. Mike Bree remembers the gas van in Penzance:

My uncle was caretaker at the town hall and he and some other workmen had been given plans and materials to erect a kind of wooden hut on wheels which had several compartments inside with a door at each end and with a door in each dividing wall. After this had been completed and painted inside and out it was still some time before he learned just what it was they had made. He was told it was a 'gas hut' for testing gas masks.

It was where we were given sniffs of small phials of the irritant type gasses; each phial heated and broken by our benevolent instructor, with suitably satanic glee and diabolical humour, over a small burner in the inner sanctum through which we filed.

It went something like this: Squad waits outside, some expectantly, others rather anxiously. Doors open and instructor tells us to file inside first room and stand back around walls so that he can stand in central space to call the roll and explain the procedure. Room 1 is just that; a bare space with a bare wooden chair in the middle. We do as instructed and 'boss-man' uses chair to support one large boot while elevated knee supports clipboard with various sheets of paper held thereon. He waits for 'ush and then checks said 'roll'.

Satisfied that we are all present and correct as detailed, he then goes into his practiced spiel about the irritant effects of certain gases on eyes, nose, throat, lungs, etc., naming those known to be in use at the time, and the skin irritant and burning effects of the splash-type gases we had heard of from the Great War and their effects on eyes and lungs that had affected so many we knew. He then ran through the various smells we could associate with these gases.

He then went on to explain that before we went in to the next room he would check the fitting/gas-tightness of our respirators and then we would file into the next room where we would test them with a sample of gas – perfectly harmless – and we would be required to do a few simple tasks.

Since we had all worn these things many times on various silly exercises from time to time, we knew they were all right, and so he found them – but, like all instructors, he had to make some 'little-bitty' alterations here and there! Then he explained that we would go next door with our respirators in position and stand, as we were now, around the walls, ensuring that the door into the next room was

Street fire parties training to use stirrup pumps in an ARP depot. You can pick out the warden trainer (centre rear) in front of the ARP gas van. (Lewisham Local Studies)

kept clear, and being careful, with our misted-up vision, not to kick over the small burner on a stand with the gauze dish on its top, and his chair nearby.

He went first through the door and signalled us to follow after. We shuffled in to find this new room very dimly lit – and it was not just the mist on our eyepieces; the only light came from the small burner flame and the red-hot wire gauze above it. As our eyes adjusted to the reduced light we saw him take a small glass phial from a cardboard box, hold it near the apparatus for a moment, then place it on the wire over the flame. Immediately a thin spiral of smoke twisted upwards, slowly, into the darker area of the ceiling. Fascinated, we watched, as we would have stared at a cobra in the wicker basket of the snake charmer as it writhed and swayed.

His Nibs allowed this smoke to finish completely its hypnotic act, then he stood and signalled us to start marking time on the spot – Guards parade stuff – and moved over to stand by the wall as we did. He then resumed his former position and signed for us to do squat bends, up and down; these were followed by signs for us to march around, as we were, in circles, round and round, which we did for a few turns of the hut. He then signalled us to stand where we were while he went to a corner of the hut, returning with a previously prepared, large-lettered, printed board which read: 'As I let you go, shout out your name, address, religion, workplace and wait for the door to open.'

By this time we were absolutely cooked and gasping for air in our clammy, sweat-lined respirators in this claustrophobic sweat-box – and could barely wait our turn to get out into that next room and take the damn things off!

What we, poor mugs, did not realise was that we had been well and truly 'conned'. The whole mystic routine had been a cunning ploy. When we lurched into the next room and ripped our masks off our sweating skulls, shouted our ludicrous instructions and waited for chief tormentor's henchman to leisurely spring the trap – we had inhaled a goodly few whiffs of the residual gas fumes he had let out into the last room when he crossed to the room while our visions were blurred and opened our door for a short while! All designed so that we would not fail to take in a few good whiffs of none-too-harmful CAP (a non-lethal tear gas).

One by one we lurched and burst from the exit door, gasping, gagging, eyes streaming, to stagger or collapse on the nearest piece of grass.

This one experience taught me more than one valuable lesson; I learned to recognise CAP gas – I also learned to be very cautious of the assurances of those in authority. The latter was to stand me in much better stead than the former.

To train so many people in a short time was a vast undertaking. Unlike the fire brigades, which also had a vast influx of new members to train, they had no 'old-timers' who could pass on their skills to the new members – even the trainers had to be trained. To this end the Ministry opened two ARP schools, one at Falfield, as early as 1936, and one at Easingwold in 1937. Here they trained the trainers;

The Fire Service College, previously the Ocean Hotel, Saltdean, Sussex. The name of the hotel on the canopy has been removed as part of the anti-invasion measures.

WAFS recruits receiving training in the use of the stirrup pump. Notice their bluette overalls.

local officers attended courses and, on successfully passing, became instructors who, on return to their local authority, would train local instructors. Often local or regional schools would be set up for this. Sometimes schools were established for specific purposes, such as the regional rescue party schools, set up in 1940 for the training of rescue party leaders, or foremen, and their deputies. In autumn 1941, the National Fire Service College was opened in the Ocean Hotel, Saltdean, which was taken over for the purpose.

PC Hugh Learmont completed his training just before the start of the war:

I went on a training course around the end of 1938 and passed it, thereby becoming an official instructor. I did not volunteer, but was just ordered to do this job by my sergeant. For giving a lecture in your own time you were paid the magnificent sum of half a crown.

We had a 16mm projector which was used in schools during the evenings to show War Department films to the public. To show our authority a lapel badge was provided as, when we were giving talks to civilian fire watchers, we were not in uniform; it was marked 'ARP Instructor'.

I and two other constables gave the demonstrations I have described and this continued until 1943, when I was promoted sergeant.

Early in that year training officers had been appointed to each region, and from June a series of training bulletins were produced, along with training films and training manuals. All these were supported by numerous commercially produced books, such as *Tactical Training in ARP for Wardens and other Civil Defence Services.*

By 1941, inter-service training, especially of rescue, decontamination and first aid parties, was carried out by leaders of the appropriate services. This meant that rescue training of decontamination squads was carried out by suitably trained rescue leaders, and had extended to the point where suitable personnel of the three services were able to assist in the work of another service, so relieving the problem of shortages.

In early 1942, the Civil Defence Staff College opened in Surrey. Here officers and officials from all the services, including the police, fire service, WVS and public utilities, received training in organisation and administration.

" Would you mind paying attention, Mrs. Eglethorpe, please : I hope you don't think they enclose directions with the bomb . . ."

Langdon cartoon. The stirrup pump is clearly illustrated, and the trainer is in early uniform – badge and armband. (Random House)

Once basic training had been completed, teams were kept up to scratch by extended training and exercises. These were usually small scale, but from time to time there would be large-scale local exercises, not only useful for training, but a good advertisement for the services, encouraging fresh volunteers and increasing local interest. These usually involved volunteer 'casualties', suitably made up; in Gloucester they went one better. In their CD record it tells how, in 1943, a squad of about a dozen wardens, all trained first aiders, acted as casualties. They spent many hours perfecting horrific mock wounds and symptoms, and proved useful for training wardens, ambulance and first aid personnel. 'As an example of the realism brought into the exercises by these means, it may be mentioned that one lady member of the team was so good at feigning hysteria that she was, on more than one occasion, very roughly handled by wardens in their efforts to calm her!'

In 1943 the Ministry of Home Security suggested that each region set up a regional training school. In the same year fire guard instructors' courses were set up in Easingwold and Falfield, where local instructors were also trained.

As the war came to a close, so did Civil Defence training, which officially ceased in December 1944.

CHAPTER 5

Control of the ARP Services

There were several levels of command of the ARP. At the top was the Minister of Home Security, based in a war room in the basement of the Home Office. He, and ministers in charge of other departments, such as Food, Transport, and Information, sat together on the Cabinet Civil Defence Committee. In 1939 the government appointed Sir John Anderson, former chairman of the ARP Committee, as joint Home Secretary and Minister of Home Security, effective on the outbreak of war. He was to have a senior civil servant as principal officer, whose deputies were to be the head of the ARP department and the inspector general of ARP. In October 1940, Sir John was replaced by Herbert Morrison, formerly head of the LCC and member of the Labour Party's ARP Committee.

Next came the twelve regional commissioners who were directly responsible to the Minister of Home Security. They were charged by Royal Warrant to ensure that the regional plans of the departments responsible for ARP and those of local authorities were properly co-ordinated. In August 1938, soon after Sir Warren Fisher recommended a regional organisation, several regional commissioners were appointed. Just one month later came the Munich Crisis, and the commissioners received orders to set up regional headquarters. The ARP inspectors, whose job had been to oversee and advise on local ARP schemes, were reorganised into regional officers based at the regional HQ, with the senior regional officer taking administrative charge of its war room. The regional officers' tasks still included advising local authorities on ARP schemes and monitoring the progress of these schemes, but to these were added the job of increasing public awareness of air raid precautions.

Each commissioner had a deputy and an HQ staff including technical advisers – engineers whose task included giving information and advice on topics such as the design of posts, trenches and shelters. Part of the regional HQ was the Regional Control Room. This required full administration and clerical staffs, including intelligence and communications officers, telephonists, clerks and messengers. Later, after the start of the Baedeker raids, staff from regional HQ were sent to towns which had suffered a large raid. There they would set up an advance regional HQ to report back to regional HQ and co-ordinate post-raid work.

The role of the regional commissioners was primarily to co-ordinate the work of the authorities within their region and the various government departments. This included presiding over the Regional Council, made up of representatives of the local authorities and regional representatives of the

Ministries of Health, Labour, Food, and Pensions, the Unemployment Assistance Board, and the Office of Works. In war, the commissioner was responsible for summoning reinforcements from other regions, or from the military. Should communications with the Ministry of Home Security break down, the commissioner would take control of his region and exercise full powers of civil government until central control was restored. To facilitate this, branch offices of all the ministerial departments concerned with ARP were stationed near each regional office.

The London, Home Counties, Scottish and Welsh regions were split up into districts, each under a District Commissioner. London, as the expected main target, had a senior regional commissioner and two regional commissioners. In these and all other regions, the next level down was the county. Counties were split into divisions,

The Town Hall—I

The Town Hall—II

Cartoon by Fougasse. The central position of the town hall in the local ARP organisation is clearly illustrated here with many of the activities that took place there in the early days.

and divisions into areas, each under an area controller, based in area HQ. This example is from the City of Gloucester's record of civil defence: '. . . it was agreed that Gloucester City should form part of Area No. 1, one of seven areas into which the whole county was to be divided for ARP purposes. Area 1 comprised the City and the Rural Districts of Gloucester, Newent and East Dean.' The London Region was split into nine groups, each containing several areas. These consisted of the inner areas, one to five, and the outer areas, six to nine. Each group came under a group controller, based at a group HQ.

The front line unit of ARP was the local 'scheme-making authority'. This referred to the ARP scheme required under the 1937 Act. These scheme-making authorities were usually the local rural or urban district councils. To oversee the implementation of local schemes, the ARP department appointed several inspectors, with Wing Commander Hodsall becoming inspector general of the ARP.

Locally, scheme-making authorities had been advised, as early as 1936, to appoint ARP organisers to oversee their schemes. As the schemes began to take shape, the work of the ARP organiser diminished, and the post was superseded by that of ARP officer, or ARPO, whose position was that of full-time administrator.

Chief ARPOs, usually the local chief constable, were appointed to co-ordinate the work of the ARPOs in their district, and the ARP organisers were taken on to their staffs. As the ARP services grew, so the administration grew and in January 1939, the ARP department advised local authorities to appoint group co-ordinating officers to relieve hard-pressed ARPOs.

The central figure in the local ARP organisation was the ARP controller. The controller, often the clerk to the council or some other council official, was appointed by the local authority, but had to be approved by the region. He was the main channel for government instructions, information and guidance on ARP matters, either directly or through the regional commissioner. He was also responsible for overseeing the co-operation of the various ARP services, and for securing co-ordination with other services, such as the police and fire brigades. This would be done by the controller or deputy controller from their HQ – the Control, or combined Report and Control, Centre.

King and queen visit Hull, August 1941. The man on the left wearing the helmet and the wing collar is the local controller, identified by the writing on his helmet. Helmets were standard issue, but not wing collars! (Hull Central Library)

The report and control centres were the local hub of ARP and other emergency services. Without them, any attempt to deal with the damage and casualties caused by even an average-sized raid would soon deteriorate into complete chaos. They were so vital to the local organisation that entrances to the centres were often guarded, and admission only granted on production of special identity cards, to foil possible sabotage attempts by fifth columnists.

Report Centres

Instructions for the arrangements for the control and co-ordination of the ARP general services at a local level were set out in ARP memorandum No. 6, issued in April 1938. If lives were to be saved, it was vital that the various services were co-ordinated, and that help was directed to the most serious incidents rather than the first one to occur, or the one nearest to the depot. For this reason, all incidents had first to be reported, usually by a warden or policeman, to the local authority's report centre; wardens were not allowed to run to the nearest service depot, no matter how close it was.

In March 1939, an ARP circular laid out the organisation of the report centres: in some larger towns there were to be several report centres, on a rough ratio of about one centre to every 100,000 of the population. In rural districts, thinly populated but spread over a large area, there were to be a series of report posts.

The function of the report centre was to receive, sift and collate all information. Often a single incident would be reported by several different individuals and due to vagueness, and/or inaccuracy, might appear to be several different incidents in the same area. Multiply this by several incidents, and it soon becomes clear how the control centre could be swamped with reports, making an accurate overview of how best to utilise the limited rescue, first aid and decontamination parties almost impossible. So the report centre's main task was to turn the incoming raw information into an accurate picture, enabling the control centre to respond appropriately.

To this end, report centres were staffed continuously on a shift basis. Staff mainly consisted of telephonists under a message room supervisor. There were also plotters, plotting clerks and chart writers. These would plot incidents on to a large map, plus other information essential to effective rescue, such as blocked roads, damaged water or gas mains, and bridges or railway lines which were impassable. The numbers of parties available at different depots would be displayed on a plotting board. Any messages concerning fires had to be passed on to the fire brigade. Similarly damage to essential services had to be notified to the appropriate public utility company. It was the duty of the executive officer (the officer in charge of the report centre) to ensure that all this was done. Several messengers would be on call in case communications broke down.

Control Centres

The nerve centre of Civil Defence was the Control Centre. The controller and the heads of the various ARP general services were based here, together with a large staff which included telephonists, clerks and messengers, plus liaison

Report and Control Centre. Of particular interest are the rank bars and stripes. The man with the single broad bar is probably the ARPO, and the woman with three narrow bars his deputy. Note also the two shoulder flash variations: Control, and Report and Control. (Kent Messenger Group Newspapers)

officers from the police, fire brigade, public utilities and, after May 1940, the Home Guard.

At first control centres were set up in any available building – Mike Bree was a messenger in Penzance:

The main police station was located in the ground floor of the town hall. It served, at its outset, as the ARP nerve-centre because it had its own telephone switchboard. At that time there were, of course, no walkie-talkie radios, or car-borne or man-pack radios for communication; all messages were carried by telephone, or written. The fire station was just a few yards away from the town hall, the police station, the ambulance garage and the light and heavy rescue squads and decontamination units also found themselves based in the town hall. The whole of the main group of services were thus conveniently handy to the Ops Room. (But not so convenient should the town hall have suffered a few direct hits.)

As the war wearied on and the various organisations grew and improved in effectiveness, the Civil Defence centre of operations to which our centre was subject was moved to a large house set in a park, now a museum, and just feet from a garden of remembrance. Here we sat in a corridor that smelled of antiquity, dust and wax polish, on rock-hard, wooden chairs, listening to the constant buzz of telephones and subdued human chatter as reports of incidents, appeals for assistance, flowed in, and as messengers of all sorts bustled in and out. We waited, on edge, for our own summons, not knowing where we would have to go, or what we might have to do to get there.

Using similar charts and maps to those in the report centre, the controller or his deputy could watch the situation developing in their area. Likewise the heads of service could despatch parties from their various posts and depots to where they were most needed, and public utilities could send out their specialist emergency repair squads. The public utilities group included parties for the repair of roads, sewers, gas, water, electricity and telephones. Each was represented at control, either by its own officers, or the district or county surveyor. Also stationed at the control centre was a gas identification officer in case of a poison gas attack.

From the control centre the controller could bring into operation the relevant rest centres for those victims who survived, and emergency mortuaries for those who did not. If the situation became such that the services available became swamped, the controller was responsible for seeking reinforcements, either locally or from neighbouring areas (this was known as mutual support), or from the region, via regional control. From November 1940, controllers could call directly for any military help available from local camps, barracks, etc., as well as the local Home Guard.

Deptford Control Room showing area map, a chart showing availability and displacement of the local services and a list of wardens' posts. (Lewisham Local Studies)

Deptford Control Centre, July 1941. Telephonists in Report and Control Centres were rarely issued with uniforms. (Lewisham Local Studies)

From the incoming information, the control centre made up reports on the local situation: damage to property and services, and casualties, which were relayed to regional headquarters, where they were used to compile regional reports. These were sent to the Ministry of Home Security and then to the Cabinet. So at every level, an accurate picture of the situation in the area was always available to local officers, and continually updated. These reports were called Damage Reports and Situation Reports. They were supplemented by Siren, First Bomb, and First Flare Reports, whose content is self-explanatory, and which gave the earliest notice of where attacks were happening.

The controller also had to decide which unexploded bombs, mines or missiles needed priority attention, and to this end would liaise with the military authorities, usually the Royal Engineers. Parachute mines, sometimes called land mines, were converted sea mines. It is rather strange, albeit logical, that these were therefore the responsibility of the naval bomb disposal units.

Report and control centres were often situated in the same building, usually the basement of the town hall or some other local authority building. In the larger districts there were subcontrol centres under subcontrollers, and in all areas emergency control centres were kept on standby in case the control centre was knocked out. A typical control centre staff consisted of about 100 men and women, mostly telephonists, divided into six shifts, each under an executive officer, taking day duty once every six days and night duty once in six nights. Both report and control centres had to be manned 24 hours a day, every day of the year.

The City of Gloucester's Civil Defence record has this to say about their control room shifts:

Except for the co-ordination between Executive Officers by means of the Controller's Staff meetings, each control shift was independent of the others and knew little of their procedure or activities. Hence it happened that with the same duties to perform in an emergency, the same background of training to undergo in preparation for it, and with similar constitutions in that a large proportion of the members of each were in various branches of the Corporation staff, it was somewhat remarkable how distinctive was the character of each of the six shifts; in fact it was almost possible to determine the number of the shift by the nature of their occupations whilst standing in. On one evening a sedate seriousness reigned, on another a distinct joviality; sometimes, after the exercise, discussion, or other form of training was finished, almost all the members could be found busily engaged at the billiard, table tennis, or card tables, at other times conversation was the rule, or the members were to be found – or not to be found – in various parts of the premises; one shift regularly enjoyed a full cooked meal, another disdained to cook at all.

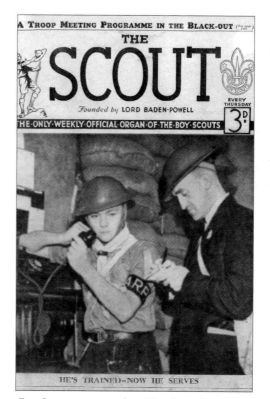

Boy Scout messenger from The Scout *magazine, 9 October 1939. The same issue carried an article on 'A troop meeting programme in the black-out'. Soon afterwards the authorities, worried about youngsters being injured, discontinued the use of young messengers except for post-raid work.*

Obviously it was imperative that communications to and from report and control centres remained open but bombing could easily disrupt telephone lines. To try to overcome this, centres had direct telephone lines to each other and the various depots, posts, etc., plus separate lines through distant exchanges, in case the local exchange were destroyed or put out of action. If all else failed, there were always the messengers.

Messengers

It was certain that even a small bombing raid would result in the disruption of services, including the telephone service. Underground cables and pipes would be severed, telegraph poles brought down and, in some cases, exchanges hit. In these eventualities messages would have to be sent by a system of runners or messengers.

At first, these messengers were part of the different services; wardens' messengers were usually chosen from local youth groups such as the Boy Scouts or Boys' Brigade, but soon after the start of the war the Government became concerned about possible casualties among youngsters and directed authorities to replace them with older volunteers, usually between the ages of fifteen and eighteen. Younger volunteers, known as Young Citizens, were used as messengers in post-raid work. Formed into pools, usually based in schools, they were called the Aftermath Messenger Service.

Messengers were required for all the services, as well as at rest centres, control centres, emergency mortuaries and so on. It was inefficient to have each service recruiting and organising their messengers separately, so in June 1941 the Civil Defence Messenger Service was established. This set up pools of messengers, based in depots or posts, who could be called upon to work where needed. During a raid, messengers would work as individuals or in small groups at the disposal of report and control centres. In 1943, this led to an extension of the control structure of the messenger service; previously, there had only been one official position of authority, that of the officer-in-charge of the service. Messengers had taken orders from the person in charge of the post or party to which they had been attached; in larger authorities it was

Margaret Cook, messenger, about 1944. She is wearing late pattern, printed shoulder flashes, and the single stripe of a senior messenger. Just visible below the CD breast badge is her local area, Southend-on-Sea.

now suggested that messengers be organised into squads of 25, under a senior messenger. Four to six squads made up a section, under a head messenger, and four sections made up a group, under a group messenger leader. Civil Defence Training Bulletin no. 10 pointed out that 'difficulties might result from placing a boy or girl in charge of a squad containing adults', but also that 'the grant of stripes in suitable circumstances to boys and girls should be regarded as an integral part of the scheme on account of the stimulus it is likely to offer to good service'.

Mike Bree recalls joining the service:

When the national call went out for more ARP workers I was not quite old enough to become a full member of the First Aid Party section, but then someone (and I still have no idea just who) came up with the idea of a National Messenger Service – and I was eligible for that at least. Despite my mum's fears that her only son was about to be blown to bits by Hun airmen, I volunteered and was accepted. With my knowledge of, and experience in, the St John Ambulance Brigade, I was automatically attached to our First Aid Party. For this the only uniform issued was a steel helmet and respirator plus an ARP badge and, a little later, a navy-blue armband which bore, printed in yellow the words 'CIVIL DEFENCE'. I was allocated to our HQ, reporting at each alert to the Police Station, on stand-by to run, or rather cycle, any messages that might need delivery, anywhere within our appointed sector. Our HQ was initially in the St John Ambulance HQ/garage in the car park at the Town Hall.

For their normal work and exercises the members of the First Aid Parties were issued overalls of dark navy. Before too long, as organisation and supplies improved, battledress in navy-blue serge became standard issue, for adults that is; for we lesser mortals, being smaller but still growing, this was not practical, so we had to wear our own clothes, at a time when replacement was hardly possible. I was lucky though in that the womenfolk in my family had been taught dressmaking and my uncle had plenty of ex-RN boiler suits of the right colour, so I had a few cut down and altered. The steel hat with which I was issued was obviously an ex-army job, still painted khaki, which I had to paint and stencil – matt black paint, white letter – at my own expense. Many did, at first, get the Great War type respirator as issued to the armed services, with separate headpiece and filter box, joined by a flexible tube, but after Dunkirk, these were needed to re-equip the services, and a rubber, moulded face piece type, with integral filter, was issued to ARP personnel.

In some areas, messengers were given bicycles by the local authority – and pretty cranky some were by all accounts – while those fortunate enough to own their own preferred to use them, as I did. Riding through broken glass, brick-rubble, debris, or across country, where necessary, wrought havoc on tyres and tubes, and punctures were frequent.

With buildings falling and blocking or partially blocking roads and streets, it was evident that most of the larger and swifter forms of transport would be slowed down – even halted – but the cyclist would still, with luck, wend his/her way and, if impeded, could even pick up the bike, sling it over a shoulder and climb over/around an obstacle, negotiate webs of fire hoses etc.,

Winston Churchill inspects bicycle messengers, Hull. The messenger on the left is wearing a fibre helmet, identified by the wavy line at the top. (Hull Central Library)

and get messages through from post to post, or from HQ downwards. Also self-evident was the simple fact that smaller cyclists were likely to be more agile/nimble than some of the larger ones. Many messengers were, of course, Boy Scouts or from other boys' organisations, but there were also some Girl Guides and other girls, I believe.

I became a messenger with several of my SJAB mates who were also school chums of several years and also lived in my near neighbourhood. Some stayed with the First Aid Parties while others were detailed to some of the other organisations.

At the outset we had no proper air raid shelter as such but a number of our masters were ex-Great War wallahs and a set of trenches were dug into which we were all supposed to file at every alert. Bad enough in high summer, but in wet and woolly winter? An air raid shelter of sorts was built in April 1940, but I never used it because, as a messenger, I had to take a cycle, tin hat and respirator (ARP type issue), to school every day and keep the last two handy. In the event of an alert, I was off to report to the centre, there to do what was required until released to return – not necessarily at the all-clear.

We lads were approaching our final time at school and our School Certificate exams, which could have quite a bearing on our future careers. Our duties were not allowed to affect things like homework. True, this was often done on duty – especially later, when we were allowed to work occasional all-night duty shifts, for which we received a small payment! No matter had the town been bombed, and we also, as well as machine-gunned on occasions, excuses were NOT accepted and failure to turn in work as requested invariably brought retribution.

Depots

Apart from wardens, who were stationed in a myriad of local posts, most of the other services, rescue parties, decontamination squads, first aid parties and emergency ambulances, were provided with transport, and were collectively known as the Civil Defence Mobile Services. They were stationed at depots, where the personnel, their equipment and vehicles could be kept until directed to

Stretcher party depot, Deptford Park School, August 1941. The 'make do and mend' nature of early ARP is well illustrated here. Evacuation meant that many school buildings were either completely or partly available for alternative uses. The stretcher party car is an adapted private car with its mudguards painted white for added visibility in the blackout, as is the SP masked headlight. (Lewisham Local Studies)

Recreation and sports room in an ARP depot, August 1941. Both party leaders are wearing early red rank stripes. (Lewisham Local Studies)

an incident by control. Set up in any convenient building – schools, garages, large houses – depots were spread around a local authority's area so that an incident anywhere could be reached with minimal delay.

Margaret Cook was a senior messenger in Southend-on-Sea; she describes her depot.

> Houses were commandeered and set up for occupation, one for the boys and one for the girls. There were only the bare necessities; table, chairs, arm-chairs, cooker, pots and pans, etc., in the kitchen, where we cooked ourselves whatever we had brought along for supper.
>
> About a dozen bunk beds and bedding were placed in two bedrooms, one single bed and a telephone in a small bedroom was for whoever was in charge who took the calls and woke up the girls to go to their posts if the siren went. It went most nights, in fact. The idea was, that when the siren went, we all pedalled like mad to our various posts, i.e. police station, fire station, ARP posts, public shelters and so on. If, for any reason, communications were disrupted, we took messages to these main points.

Depots usually contained facilities for preparing food, training and sleeping, as well as communications with control. Often depots were 'combined': shared by two or

Early mixed depot. There is a very interesting range of helmets on display, including first aid party with party number (A2), and the Depot Superintendent (D Supt). Unfortunately the plus fours were not uniform issue. (Kent Messenger Group Newspapers)

more services. Depots were usually commanded by a depot superintendent who was in charge of administration. This included drawing up the daily programme of training, exercises and recreation. Recreation included physical training and organised sports such as football and boxing. Other facilities, such as snooker tables, wireless sets and dartboards were provided for those on rest periods. Discussion groups were set up, led by specially selected and trained volunteers.

Incident Officers

Once the bombing started in earnest it soon became clear that control of large incidents was rarely satisfactory. There were so many parties from different services, with equipment and transport, that they were bound to get in each other's way; communication and co-operation often broke down, and co-ordination was difficult. A system of incident officers began to evolve, based on the experiences of several local authorities. One, in London, was introduced in November 1939 for serious incidents, in which a warden would take overall control at the site, and would then be known as the incident officer.

In May 1940, Operations and Training Manual no. 4 was introduced. It dealt with the direction and control of police, fire and ARP services at incidents. It said that each service should continue to work under the control of its own officers, but that co-ordination of the various services should be the responsibility of the police. Where several services were involved at an incident, the senior police officer present should set up an 'incident post', at which he, and the senior officer of each service present, could always be contacted.

As the war continued, it became obvious that the police were overstretched and this was one task too many. Police schools for incident control training began to accept wardens on their courses.

In May 1943 it was agreed that incident officers should form a separate Civil Defence service, normally under the control of the chief constable, although once at the incident they came under the ARP controller. Two months later a memorandum was issued which superseded Manual no. 4. This said that each scheme-making authority should have a pool of trained incident officers consisting of 'Police officers, wardens and other selected persons', and that other wardens and police officers should be partially trained in incident control, to be able to work at an incident until the incident officer arrived or, in the case of a smaller incident, to take control throughout.

It was never the job of the incident officer to tell the specialist teams how to do their job. The incident officer's task was to co-ordinate the activities of the various services present, and to act as the on-the-spot representative of the controller, relaying situation reports to him and transmitting his instructions to the service officers present. The incident officer therefore needed to have a team of messengers on hand. Noel Care joined the ARP in Hastings soon after the Munich Crisis, at the age of sixteen:

My dad was a warden, I was made a messenger, but I had a deformed hand, and because of this I could not ride a bicycle, so I was made an Incident Post Messenger. This meant that at large incidents I would run messages for the Incident Officer. This was usually a policeman, but sometimes if a senior officer from Control was free, he would be sent to do the job.

I was working in a small grocers about 150 yards from the centre of the town. A bomb had been heard (luckily this one landed in the sea), and my manager said, 'off you go', so I left to go to control, only five minutes hurried walk. I went past a small cinema at the town centre. I passed a word or two with the manager who I knew quite well; 50 yards on I turned left. I was only about 15 yards further on when the bomb hit. It actually hit the coping of the cinema and killed the manager among many others. I was back at the incident about a quarter of an hour later working.

The incident post would be set up near a priority telephone, often at a warden's post. All party or squad leaders would report to this incident post on arrival to receive instructions, and would usually base themselves there. Obviously it was important that the IP should be instantly recognisable and, to this end, IPs were marked with a flag, usually blue and white check, during the day, and by coloured lamps at night. For the same reason, IOs were distinguishable by a sky-blue cloth helmet cover, and/or a sleeve badge bearing the letters IO. On-the-spot service leaders set up 'action posts' near to the IP and these were also marked by special flags and lamps.

As the incident came under control the IO, under the direction of the controller, would release parties for return to their depots or for despatch to another incident.

Incident Inquiry Points

One of the problems faced by those working at incidents was dealing with the general public. Some would be anxiously seeking information about missing friends and relatives, some would be bombed out, or their homes damaged; others would be seeking advice or trying to give information about those missing. Many would be distressed or confused and needed calm and sympathetic handling; obviously not a job for the hard-pressed incident officer.

Various schemes were adopted to overcome this; in Gloucester, for example, all possible information was collected and held at wardens' posts close to the incident, and enquiries directed there, but this scheme had several drawbacks. The *Incident Control Manual*, issued in 1943, suggested that a responsible warden or member of the WVS be put in charge of an incident inquiry post

Police incident officer with party leaders. Behind them is the chequered incident post flag. (Hull Central Library)

or point, sited near but not too close to the incident. All enquiries and reports from members of the general public could then be directed there, keeping the area around the incident clear, and allowing the incident officer to get on with his or her job. The first IIP was set up at St Pancras in October 1943. By the beginning of 1944, the WVS had completely taken charge of setting up and running IIPs.

The manual proposed that an IIP be set up at the direction of the incident officer, and that it should remain open until the controller, on the advice of the incident officer, decided that it had served its purpose. The manual added that the point should be established conveniently close to the incident post, so that the two could keep in constant contact, and that the IIP should be clearly marked. This was at first done with a poster designed by the WVS and later with a metal sign marked 'INCIDENT INQUIRY POINT', illuminated at night by a warden's hand-lamp. Experience soon showed that a minimum of four people were needed to operate an IIP; a 'receptionist', an interviewer, a recorder and a clerk to deal with incoming information. It was normal to supplement these with messengers, escorts and often people to supply refreshments.

IIPs were set up in any convenient position – the front room of a nearby house, a shop, a school, or even just a table on the pavement. In the four weeks from mid-June 1944, during the flying-bomb assault, over 750 IIPs were set up in various parts of London alone – in fact, they became so useful that several boroughs set up mobile IIPs in specially adapted vans.

One of the later Civil Defence innovations, the IIPs proved a great success. They not only served the purposes outlined above but many others, and the information they received from the public as to the whereabouts of 'missing' people saved the rescue service hours of wasted work.

Observation Points

From the earliest days, great attention had been paid to enemy flares as they were usually followed by incendiary or HE bombs. Consequently, wardens were directed to report the dropping of flares immediately to control – the first flare report. This had the effect of swamping control as all local wardens sent in their reports, so they began to be filtered out by wardens' posts or, if it existed in the local area, wardens' HQ. To allow a more accurate plotting of where the flares were being dropped, many areas set up suitably protected 'Observation Posts', usually placed on high buildings or hills, where the flares could not only be observed but their bearings noted, and thus, by triangulation, the area under threat identified. Some of these OPs were part of wardens' posts, and were therefore staffed by wardens; others by the NFS, although often only during alerts. As with the Observer Corps, who kept constant watch for approaching enemy aircraft, the job called for constant alertness. Where posts were covered full-time, a rota of six, on a two-on, four-off basis was the usual system.

Later, during the V-weapon assault, they were able to identify the fall of the bombs and rockets, and summon the rescue, fire and casualty services with minimum delay.

Bomb Reconnaissance Officers

Not all bombs went off. Some were faulty, and others were delayed action (DA) bombs, which were designed to go off some time after they had fallen. Together these were called unexploded bombs, or UXBs as they became known.

Frank Padgham, a Southsea fireman, recalls a UXB:

One night the sirens were sounded and we were sent to Taswell Road; as we arrived we heard the now-familiar whistle – we waited – there was a loud crash but no explosion. A lady came rushing out of a house further down the street, shouting for help. We went back with her and there in the front room was a large hole, while above us we could see the sky. We looked down the hole and by the light of our torches we could see the fin of a very large unexploded bomb. We beat a hasty retreat and after making sure that everyone in the area was notified we waited for the bomb disposal team. What brave chaps they were – they got to work on it and we learnt that it was a 500 lb HE, and that if it had gone off it would have caused considerable casualties, including us!

ARP exercise: 'And how long have you been a casualty?' An air raid 'casualty' is questioned by London Regional Commissioner Admiral Sir Edward Evans. The admiral is wearing a yellow version of the CD armband as issued to senior regional and ministry officials.

UXBs and objects suspected of being UXBs caused huge disruption as streets and buildings had to be sealed off, sometimes for days. Often these objects proved to be nothing more than a pipe or a piece of debris, as in the *Just William* story, 'William Carries On'. It was therefore vital that local officers could investigate suspect objects and decide which were real.

In September 1939 a circular asked local authorities to provide a small number of volunteers to be trained to protect the public from UXBs. Those successfully completing the course were to become 'bomb reconnaissance officers' (BROs). The scheme came to nothing, but from early in 1941 a few places on military bomb recognition courses were available to ARP personnel who, upon their return, could train wardens in their local area. In some areas, the trained wardens were called 'bomb recognition wardens'. While many BROs were wardens, a sizeable minority were police officers, and even Fire Guard officers.

CHAPTER 6

Reinforcements

Even before the war the ARP Department had recognised that bombing was likely to be localised; one town or borough would be suffering from a heavy raid, stretching its Civil Defence services to breaking point, while its neighbours might have the odd scattered bomb, or no action at all. The answer to this was a system of mutual support among neighbouring areas, and even further afield. In 1940 a training manual entitled *Reinforcement* was issued, brought up to date by a second edition in 1942, which incorporated the lessons learnt in the big blitz and the invasion scares.

The arrangements for mutual support between neighbouring areas were left to those areas to sort out, but the details had to be communicated to the regional commissioner so that he could take the schemes into account before working out the numbers needed for more remote reinforcements. Mutual aid, as it was called, was usually based on the group system, whereby several scheme-making authorities were banded together into a group, with a Group HQ under a group co-ordinating officer. The controller of a besieged town would request support through the Group HQ; other controllers within the group would then respond by sending what reinforcements they could, without, of course, leaving their own areas vulnerable. If the need was sufficiently large, or the damage spread over a wide area, group control might apply to the region for reinforcement.

The Civil Defence Reserve

Early in the war, Kent made the decision to set up a mobile reserve of Civil Defence workers trained in first aid, rescue work and decontamination. Three companies were set up, each of 200 personnel. Other counties soon followed suit and, in July 1941, the Ministry of Home Security formalised things by setting up the Civil Defence Reserve, made up of mobile reserve units from each region. Units were normally made up of three to five operational groups of 40–50 members each, plus a staff group, all under a commandant. Each operational group comprised four general utility parties of about ten, including a leader and a driver. Extra personnel included ambulances and their staff, and messengers, including despatch riders. In October 1944, an Overseas Column was set up. This unit did post-raid work, especially in Antwerp, as well as training local groups.

Regional Columns

Reinforcements between regions were often carried out by Regional Columns. These consisted of about 120 full-time men, together with women ambulance drivers and assistants, all fully trained to undertake rescue, first aid and decontamination duties, and included the regional column reserve parties which consisted of ten men, including a driver, and were the equivalent of London's heavy rescue squads. A portion of each column was always ready to move off at a few minutes notice, travelling in convoy, under a convoy commander, made up of detachments, each under a detachment leader. Convoys would make their way to the area needing reinforcement via a series of contact points, where they would receive updated orders. This meant that, if necessary, convoys could be diverted and, at the same time, pick up guides to the next point.

Throughout each region a series of 'rendezvous points' were set up, usually near a wardens' post or public call office, so as to be easily contacted. To make

Incident officer and messenger at tea van. The IO is wearing the distinctive blue helmet cover and sleeve badge of the service; he and all the other adults are wearing the second issue uniform, while the messenger is in early bluette overalls. Also of interest is the blackout hand-lamp on the warden's belt (far right). (Imperial War Museum)

them easier to find, they were marked by blue and white striped boards by day and two blue lamps, placed side by side, at night. These were where incoming reinforcements would report, and from where they would be guided to the places where they would be deployed via their reinforcement camp. There were a series of reinforcement camps to provide bases where reinforcements could leave their personal kit, and to provide facilities for eating and sleeping.

The reinforcements were supplemented by mobile first aid units, cleansing units, mobile canteens and the Queen's Messenger Service. An early lesson of the big blitz was that after the heaviest raids, a few mobile canteens supplying tea and sandwiches were nowhere near enough; what was needed was a method to feed thousands of people for several days. These food convoys, as they were at first called, consisted of several vehicles including water and food carriers and field kitchens. They were named 'Queen's Messenger Food Convoys' after Queen Elizabeth (today's Queen Mother), who set up and donated the first of eighteen such convoys.

The first convoy to go into action was based in Lewisham. This report comes from the *Lewisham Borough News*:

LEWISHAM CONVOY AT COVENTRY

It was not until 12 o'clock on Wednesday April 9, that Mrs Griggs, Head of Lewisham's Queen's Messengers, was notified that the food convoy was wanted to go to Coventry.

By 2 o'clock the store lorries had been stacked with bread, milk, and other necessary food-stuffs. All the personnel were assembled for the journey, and the convoy was ready to set off.

As the notice was so short, many of the staff, all of whom were members of the local WVS, had had no time to get in touch with their husbands and had to leave a note for when they came in at night.

In great spirit, the convoy of four motorcyclists and eight lorries, with a complement of 27 staff, set off on their journey to the north.

They travelled the 100 miles in five hours, arriving just after 7pm. They were ordered by the Food Ministry to put up at a town safely out of the blitz area in case of another attack that night. They were given a light meal. For several, it was the first solid food they had had since breakfast that morning. After a night's sleep in their billets in a children's home, the whole convoy entered the city of Coventry at 7 o'clock in the morning.

The boilers were soon boiling, the soup made and the sandwiches cut. The convoy then split up, the three mobile canteens being sent to different parts of the city, the stores and water vans staying at the allotted pitch. All the time DA bombs kept exploding all around.

During the two days at Coventry, about 14,000 meals were served, and it was with great reluctance that they returned on Saturday afternoon, in spite of the fact that they had been on their feet the major part of the time, only snatching off moments to rest.

Later, the V-weapon assault called for smaller teams and the convoys were split up into food flying squads.

CHAPTER 7

Wardens

Air raid wardens are by far the best known of all CD workers, yet they were not part of the original structure for the ARP services. It was not until ARP memorandum no. 4 was produced in January 1937 that such an organisation was outlined. In the memorandum local authorities were told:

> Their chief duty in times of peace will be to establish contact with their fellow citizens in their sectors, and to advise them on the officially recommended precautions against air raids. In time of war, they will have to be at their posts as desired, to report immediately the particulars of air raid damage, to know how to begin relief measures and generally to assist the inhabitants.

In March of that year the formation of the ARP Wardens' Service was announced; its members continued to be called, officially, ARP wardens, and later, Civil Defence wardens, but they were known almost universally as air raid

Women wardens using stirrup pump, October 1941. The woman on the left is wearing men's issue overalls and her companion is in non-regulation overalls. (Lewisham Local Studies)

wardens, or just wardens. Memorandum no. 4 described the kind of people required: 'The intention is that an Air Raid Warden will be a responsible member of the public chosen to be a leader and adviser to his neighbours in a small area or "sector" – a street or small group of streets – in which he is known and respected.' To this end, 'Their work as Wardens will in the normal course be undertaken close to their homes or places of work.'

The warden was to be a jack of all trades, performing many jobs, as opposed to the more specialist tasks performed by the other ARP general services. Among the jobs mentioned in the memorandum were: helping to shepherd members of the public to shelter when an air raid warning is received, and assisting with casualties or damage after bombs have fallen, until skilled help arrives; affording a channel by which responsible officials can be rapidly informed of the fall of bombs in any part of the district, and the effect of the damage caused; giving immediate warning in their locality of the presence of gas; setting an example of coolness and steadiness among their neighbours, and so reducing the risk of panic and loss of morale.

In essence, the warden was the civilian equivalent of the 'beat bobby', but there were far more of them; almost half of all ARP workers (not counting the fire guard, a later addition) were wardens. It was their task to patrol their sector on a rota with other wardens – when the warning was sounded all of those not on duty would turn out. On hearing a bomb fall, they would find the incident, size up the situation and report back – indeed their foremost duty was to ensure that their report reached control. They were most certainly not to contact the other services direct; this was the job of control. Wardens were continually trained to compile and send reports using the principles of speed, accuracy, brevity and clarity.

> In *Hell's Corner 1940*, a woman warden describes her job following a house being hit:
>
> I go into a house, decide who's alive, who's dead, tot up the number of victims and what is necessary in the way of fire services, ambulances and demolition, etc. I'm quite used to seeing dead people, not perturbed by it a bit. I've got hardened to it and take it for granted.
>
> Women wardens are better than men in most cases, not all. They can see in a moment who is in the house because they know what to look for. If the kettle is on the stove they know the occupants are probably downstairs and have not gone to bed; if there is a cot, they know there is a baby about somewhere. They are better at first aid too; besides, women with their clothes blown off prefer to have another woman attending them.

Women made up one-sixth of all wardens.

When the specialist services arrived, the warden supplied them with any help or information. To this end, it was vital that wardens knew their sectors like the back of their hand; they had to know the building; who lived there, where they normally sheltered, whether they were likely to have been inside at the time of the explosion, where the stopcocks and switches and so on were located.

In terms of the local area, the warden had to know whether there were any danger spots in the surrounding area such as petrol, oil or chemical stores. Was there equipment nearby which could be useful, such as builders' stores, jacks, break-down lorries and the like? There were other simple but vital things like the position of the nearest telephone. Wardens had to know if any of the local people had special skills or knowledge which could be helpful, and who could be called on to help move rubble, look after those lightly injured, shocked, bereaved, elderly and so on, and where they were likely to be found. Wardens also had to show those who had been bombed-out or who were seeking friends or relatives the way to the nearest rest centre, first aid post or hospital.

Warden's post: the white helmet and early red bar-and-diamond rank badges on his lower forearm show the main figure to be a post warden. He also wears, against regulations, a Civil Defence armband on his overalls. It was in the early part of the war that local variations in uniforms and badges were at their height.

For this reason, and to make sure the turn-out was speedy, part-time wardens all worked in their local area. Some full-time wardens were attached to posts away from home, but their first task on arriving at their posting would be to make themselves fully knowledgeable about it.

Generally, wardens in towns were attached to sector posts, which in 1939 might be the front room of one of their houses or a shop basement. In urban areas, the aim was to have one sector post for every 500 people, the post being connected by telephone to the report centre. It soon became clear that it was not possible for the GPO to maintain so many telephones during raiding so the scheme changed; posts were established on the basis of not more than ten posts per square mile, and so arranged that, wherever an incident might occur in their area, no warden should have to go more than half a mile to make a report. It was recommended that wardens' posts should be divided into three sections. First, a protected area, shielded against blast, splinters, gas and falling debris. This area was to be provided with a telephone, table, lockers and both mains and auxiliary lighting.

The second area was the equipment store room. This would house all the wardens' equipment, which included respirators, anti-gas suits, eye shields, gloves and curtains. The latter were worn on the helmet, to protect the neck, rather like a foreign legionnaire's kepi, rather than hung at windows. Other equipment included rubber boots, electric torches, rattles for gas warning, and hand-bells for gas all-clear. The third area was the rest room. This was not an essential part of the post but it provided for those not yet on duty or those recently off duty. In the last weeks before war broke out, a large number of unused buildings were requisitioned for use as wardens' posts, but many of these proved unsatisfactory and were replaced by specially constructed permanent posts. Posts were to be constantly manned during alerts by three wardens. All were under the post warden, who was responsible for the equipment in the post, as well as for the wardens attached to it. In Camberwell, during the flying-bomb assault, many of the wardens' posts operated a scheme by which materials for 'first aid' repairs on houses were issued to householders; in the borough over 22,000 houses were damaged.

Each sector was served by at least five wardens under a senior or sector warden, with a second warden as deputy. Several sectors were covered by a wardens' post, under the control of a post warden. Several post areas made up a group under a head warden, sometimes called an area warden, who would be in charge of an area containing about 6,000–8,000 people. Larger towns (those with a population of

Wardens in anti-gas suits. Several are holding gas rattles, like large football rattles. These were used to warn of gas drops. The two outer wardens (front row) are holding hand-bells, which were used for gas all-clear. (Kent Messenger Group Newspapers)

more than 150,000) would be split up into divisions, under a divisional warden controlling eight to ten head wardens. Head, district and divisional wardens would all be supported by a deputy, so that one of them would always be on call.

At the head of the local wardens' service was the chief warden, usually based at the control centre or the wardens' headquarters. He would be supported by a deputy, and, in the early days of the service, he might also be assisted with administration, training, organisation and recruitment by a full-time paid wardens' organiser. Later, he might have training, equipment, communications and post welfare officers. He would have under his direct control a reserve of wardens to use as reinforcements.

In rural districts, however, the organisation was far less prescribed. It was intended that it should reflect the character of the local area. While the area might be far bigger than a town, bombs falling on much of it would not require the attendance of the ARP services, so wardens were concentrated in the villages. In some areas, pairs of wardens would patrol main roads by car; in others, observation posts were set up in high places, such as church towers or hill tops. Alan Barron was a warden in Hurstpierpoint:

> I served in Civil Defence in a large area just south of the Sussex Downs from November 1940 till demobilisation. I had to take a refresher course in first aid, cycling weekly to Lewes for this. I was enrolled into a roster vacancy as an ARP warden, but also in many other capacities, as a car driver, in charge of replacement of respirators for kiddies and others, working at the report centre, later also in charge of the local Fire Guards, who I had to enrol and train; also I was asked to train the girl telephonists and messengers – I used to have to escort them to and from an all-services post manned every night.

Wardens' training reflected the all-round nature of their tasks. As well as a knowledge of the ARP organisation and of the local police and fire brigades, they were trained in elementary first aid, anti-gas measures, incendiary fighting, protection against high explosive bombs and report writing. Selected wardens were sent on courses in incident control and bomb reconnaissance, and it was common for wardens to take the Royal Life Saving Society's resuscitation course, for which a special badge was issued.

Later, wardens were trained for rescue work; a training pamphlet (no. 7) was issued in 1943 under the title *Notes for the Guidance of Wardens at Rescue Incidents*. It was stressed that the warden should attempt no rescue work until their primary task of reporting was carried out. Among the advice given was: 'It is thoroughly sound practice, and one to be encouraged, to remove as much debris as possible by hand rather than by the use of tools. Where it is necessary to employ shovels, they should be used with care and only skilled persons should be allowed to work with picks in a debris pile. . . . The public will generally be useful in handling light debris or to form a chain of helpers passing back, clear of the incident, debris removed by the rescue party.' More worryingly, perhaps, it was felt necessary to add: 'Do not smoke or strike matches in case coal-gas is escaping.' and 'Avoid touching loose electric wires; they may be still alive.'

One of the crucial ways that wardens could be involved in rescue work was in the direction of members of the public in the absence of a rescue party. In these conditions it was vital to bear in mind the damage that untrained amateurs could do. Mike Bree recalls:

Any ARP worker can tell you that they have arrived at an 'incident' and found civilians already at work and often someone even organising things, without any 'official' being on hand. In the case of those buried, it soon became obvious that care in movement about the wreckage, careful removal of debris, even just a periodic pause and quiet listening – and calling out – to anyone trapped below, saved more lives and time than a bald-headed assault by the untrained. Even so, just look at some of those scenes from old photographs and see just how many obvious civilians are helping out. When the proper stretcher parties were fully extended almost anyone would handle an old door to move dead, dying, injured, or even the disabled, out of the way. Often it was necessary to improvise and remains were moved in old blankets, coats, and the like – anything handy and nearby was used.

It was the job of warden or police nearest any incident to try to keep well-meaning but unskilled rescuers away, and to look for any 'UXBs', mark the site, and keep the curious away from these too. Someone, or even, as often did happen, several people, working frantically and without co-ordination, with no real knowledge of what lay beneath and/or around them, could and in some cases did cause the 'pick-a-stick' heap of wedged timbers, stones, pieces of furniture etc., which were held together merely by the way they fell and interlocked, to collapse onto the unfortunates awaiting rescue.

One of the earliest jobs for the wardens was the fitting of gas masks. Here the male warden tests the mask for airtightness, while the womam warden (right) takes notes. The very early nature of this photo is shown not only by the complete lack of uniform but by the absence of even the lapel badge.

The first real task for the wardens was the respirator census; every man, woman, and child had to be supplied with a respirator, or gas mask, and the job of making lists of the different types and sizes required in all areas fell to the wardens. Later, in the summer of 1939, they issued the masks and helped with their adjustment. The early days of the war were taken up

Grove Park wardens' post F95, Lewisham, 1945. The red service chevrons worn on the lower right forearm help to date this picture; one was given for each year of war service. Also of interest are the range of whitehats and the W/FG (warden/fire guard) helmet, belonging to the head warden/fire guard. Note that the original metal ARP badge is still being used as a beret badge. (Lewisham Local Studies)

with the blackout, and it was at this time that wardens got a reputation as 'busybodies'. This was exacerbated by the 'phoney war' period, where Civil Defence personnel began to be seen as 'army dodgers', who spent their time playing darts.

Mike Bree said: 'In the very early days of the war, many air raid wardens earned, and thoroughly deserved, the scorn and derision they suffered because they did, regrettably, act like "Little Hitlers". Perhaps they were just too keen to do their job right; maybe, as many who suffered under their petty officiousness accused, they were suddenly "little men" given too much authority, or some were just bullies.' There were loud calls for the slimming down of the ARP services and in April 1940 the number of full-time wardens at each post was cut to two.

With the coming of serious raids in 1940 and the realisation that the incendiary bomb was such an effective weapon, it became the wardens' responsibility to form and equip street fire parties in their sectors.

One of the biggest tasks they had to undertake was the compilation of the Household Register. This contained the following information: how many people were resident in each dwelling; where each one usually slept; where they sheltered; whether any of them were deaf, disabled or elderly; the names of next of kin, and so on. Again, many saw this as unnecessary intrusion by over-officious nosey parkers, and at first many refused to co-operate, but later, when the bombs fell, the local warden was quickly able to find the occupants of a bombed house in the local public shelter, or direct the rescue party to the part of the house in which trapped occupants were sleeping, and tell them how many casualties to expect. This saved vital time and unnecessary effort by the rescuers. When the warning sounded, wardens were able to warn the deaf, or help the infirm into the shelter.

Another of their tasks was to oversee the public shelters. In some areas, part-time shelter marshals did the job at first, under the control of a chief shelter marshal, but by the end of 1940 all shelter marshals were renamed shelter wardens and came under the control of the wardens' service. Early in the following year, the wardens' service became responsible for recruiting and organising the newly formed fire guards, and one year later, head and senior wardens automatically became head and senior fire guards, in command of the fire guard in their area.

On the whole, the wardens' service was made up of men too old to join the forces – many had fought in the First World War and had been recruited through the British Legion. But women also joined, as did young men waiting to be called up.

Hell's Corner 1940 tells the following story:

One of the first of these [medal winners] was Troop Leader Donald Jones, aged eighteen, of St Margaret's Group of Boy Scouts Medway Association.

During a raid on the night of July 17th–18th, when four people were killed and nineteen injured in the Medway Towns, Troop Leader Jones, who was a warden, went to the aid of people trapped under a great deal of wreckage in their damaged house. He wormed his way beneath the timbers until his body protected the upturned faces of the two people trapped in the wreckage, and protected them from the shower of dust which resulted from every movement of the rescue party. There he remained for four hours at great danger to himself, chatting cheerfully with them until they were released.

The George Medal had not been introduced at that time, or he no doubt would have received it. But he was awarded the OBE Gallantry Medal, and also the Silver Cross of the Boy Scouts for his heroism.

At the other end of the scale, one Plymouth warden, Mr G.H. Foster, was awarded the British Empire Medal. He was 83 years old and never failed to turn out for a raid.

CHAPTER 8

Casualty Services

From the very first ARP schemes, an efficient casualty service was considered vital for the upkeep of civilian morale. The casualties were expected to be of such a scale that a system of triage was necessary. This was based on the method perfected at the front line in the First World War, where casualties were first dealt with at the front by medical orderlies. These 'medics' would deal with slight injuries on the spot, more serious injuries being sent to one of a number of aid posts set up just behind the trenches. Here doctors and their assistants would treat those they could help, while the most seriously injured were sent to a casualty clearing hospital.

This system was reflected in Civil Defence services through the use of first aid parties at an incident, then a series of first aid posts, each with a doctor and trained nurses to treat those more seriously injured. The most serious casualties would be sent on to a casualty clearing hospital.

Together, these groups, along with the emergency ambulance service, made up the ARP casualty service. After 1938, unlike most of the other services, the casualty service came under the Ministry of Health, and locally under the Medical Officer of Health, who also controlled the emergency mortuaries, food de-contamination and gas cleansing.

Each wardens' sector had a doctor attached to it who was to be summoned to an incident if there were any casualties. These were called ARP medical officers or incident doctors.

Borough Medical Officer working from headquarters. His shoulder flashes read MOH (Medical Officer of Health) and the narrow and broad stripe rank bars distinguish him as head of the Casualty Service, as do the two black stripes on his helmet.

First Aid Parties

First aid parties went directly to incidents to carry out immediate first aid on casualties, allowing those with minor injuries to go home. Those with more serious injuries could be given emergency treatment and then be sent on to first aid posts or direct to the casualty clearing hospital. In London first aid parties were called stretcher parties.

At first, personnel for the first aid parties were usually drawn from members of the St John Ambulance Brigade, the British Red Cross Society, and in Scotland, the St Andrew's Ambulance Corps. Later, like most casualty service personnel, many were trained by those societies, and all members of the first aid parties had to hold a certificate in first aid from one of them, the LCC or the Fire Brigades' Association.

Noel Care went through the training:

When I was eighteen I was transferred from the messenger service to a first aid party. No matter how much first aid training you had received, you still had to take a full first aid course immediately. Until you had passed that you could be a member of a first aid party, but if you did go out with them, you went as an extra. By this time the courses were run jointly by the Red Cross and St John's. If you were a member of one or the other you could wear their badge on your uniform after qualification. I was a member of the Red Cross so I wore their badge, a red cross on a white circle on a dark blue background, in what you might call 'World War Two embroidery'. I wore it on my right hand breast pocket.

The exact make-up of a first aid party, its equipment and so on, varied from one local authority to another. This was the organisation in Hastings: a first aid party consisted of a party car and five people (one being the party leader) – although they could, if necessary, go out with only four – a sitting case car with a female driver, and an ambulance with driver and attendant (both female). At first, all the members in the party car were male, but from 1942, women were allowed to become members. The lower age limit remained at eighteen throughout, although this was not always adhered to.

Barbara Daltrey was in a first aid party in Windsor:

I joined ARP just before war broke out; I was sixteen and a half at the time. I worked as an apprentice bookbinder in a printers, and one of the older people there got me involved. I had to take classes in first aid and when I had finished I was attached to the first aid parties. My job was to go out with the nurse on the ambulance. Our depot was a disused brewery. When on duty – I did a shift from about 10 p.m. to 6 a.m. – I slept in a damp cellar there.

When my shift finished I would cycle home for breakfast and then cycle back to work.

At first all cars used were private cars, loaned for party use, which had to be loaded when required, but later, after about mid-1943, specially converted light vans were used, which were kept permanently loaded. All members of the first

LCC converted ambulance. First aid/stretcher parties were the one CD service routinely to carry water bottles as part of their equipment. (Lewisham Local Studies)

aid party were issued with battledress, overcoat, boots, leather gaiters (these were seldom worn), steel helmet and service gas mask. Anti-gas clothing, wellington boots, boiler suits and waterproof cloaks were issued to each member, but were generally kept at the depot.

When attending an incident, each member carried a metal water bottle and a haversack containing six small, medium and large first aid dressings and six triangular bandages, thick rubber gloves and four small splints. It also contained six card labels to attach to casualties and an indelible pencil; these would be used to record specific information such as: X – internal injury, T – tourniquet fitted, and so on. The label could then be attached to the patient, or the code letter might be written on the patient's forehead, using the indelible pencil, or a lipstick, which many of the parties carried for the purpose. They also carried a pair of scissors, which most party members wore attached to a white lanyard over the left shoulder with the scissors kept in the left breast pocket when not in use.

The car carried four metal stretchers fixed on the top, eight blankets, which the party sat on, a complete set of splints and a large haversack. This contained reserve equipment including spare dressings, bandages and labels, packs of cotton wool and various small items. After each incident, each member replenished the contents of their personal haversacks from the large one, which would itself be

Stretcher party at an incident displaying a range of helmet markings. The two whitehats are a party leader (left), and a party supervisor (centre), who also wears the early, large, red rank stripes. (Lewisham Local Studies)

replenished from HQ stores on return to the depot. The large haversack also contained a Trigg lift – this was made up of four webbing straps with a metal handle at each end – and a King's harness, which was used for fixing a casualty to a stretcher, although bandages were often used for this.

As Noel Care says: 'You can imagine a small car, about the size of a Standard Eight, packed with the car equipment, five people and their personal equipment!' He goes on to illustrate the usefulness of the labels: 'I had one unfortunate incident where an untrained person used a tourniquet improperly; it did not stop the bleeding. They did not use a label or tell us and the tourniquet was covered by a blanket. By the time we found out and stopped the bleeding it was almost too late.'

The number of parties in any particular area varied; there were four categories ranging from two shifts of 33 parties per 100,000 population, in areas regarded to be of the highest risk, such as dock areas, down to the lowest risk category, of 20 parties per 100,000. First aid parties were based in depots, usually shared with rescue and ambulance personnel, and came under the immediate control of the first aid staff officer, who was on the staff of the Medical Officer of Health.

In south-east England, some members of first aid parties were forbidden to leave their areas in the event of invasion. In such an emergency, they had to report to their depot, from where they would be seconded to the Home Guard to act as their 'medics'. Combined exercises were a common occurrence as part of this plan.

Noel Care: 'Some of the parties were full-time, but mine were all part-time volunteers. I was an agricultural worker during the day. We had to report for duty as soon as the warning went, and the volunteer parties took it in turn to be on standby at the depot. Every night there was one party on standby, from ten in the evening in summer, nine in winter, until six in the morning. Normally we slept if we weren't called out, but I remember on the night before D-Day we were told to stay awake. We weren't told why, of course. The planes had to go over us and we watched them going over all night. I suppose they wanted us out in case of accidents.'

By 1942, with the problems of manpower shortages, it had become obvious that the role of the first aid parties could easily be taken on by the light rescue parties, most of whom had also been trained in first aid. Inter-service training intensified, especially between the first aid, rescue and decontamination services; leaders of the three parties would go on training courses in the work of the other two services, then return and train their own parties. In London this led to the absorption of the stretcher parties into the light rescue service, a lead that was followed in January 1943 by the rest of the country.

First Aid Posts

In general first aid posts were intended for those casualties who needed attention from a doctor, but were unlikely to need subsequent treatment. The purpose was to protect casualty hospitals from a rush of minor cases or, in the case of more

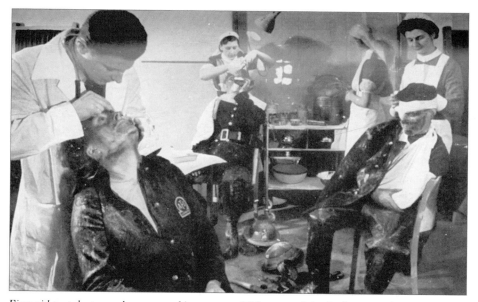

First aid post doctor and nurses working on two AFS men and, in the foreground, a WAFS driver. Fire service personnel were particularly prone to eye injuries from sparks and smoke.

The Medical Officer of Health for Croydon inpects an ARP mobile dressing station, later called a mobile first aid unit, and its staff.

serious injuries, to arrest haemorrhage and relieve pain in those who might need to receive further treatment. These injuries did not have to be the result of enemy action – many domestic and road accidents were dealt with at first aid posts.

First aid posts were staffed day and night throughout the war on a rota. A doctor was in charge of each post, aided by at least one qualified nurse and supported by a team of first aid workers of varying experience, usually trained by the St John Ambulance Brigade or Red Cross. The doctor would be responsible for the further training of the first aid workers. The size of the post's personnel was based on the size of the area it served, from small posts of about 16 staff, catering for a local population of less than 20,000, up to large posts of about 40 staff, catering for a population between 30,000 and 60,000.

There were also mobile first aid posts – specially equipped vans, containing cupboards of first aid equipment, folding operating tables and emergency lighting systems and the like, staffed by teams of experts, including a medical officer, deputy medical officer (both doctors) and trained nurses. They were usually stationed at ambulance depots and would be sent out by control to serious incidents. They would also go to incidents where there was no first aid post nearby, so that one could be set up in a suitable building in the vicinity. There were also light medical first aid units, which were cars carrying at least one doctor and two nurses, each with a medical haversack.

In addition to first aid posts, first aid points, established in private houses, libraries and so on, had at least two trained first aiders, available on a shift basis.

First aid points were set up in villages with populations of under 3,000, and in towns as a supplement to the first aid posts.

Emergency Ambulances

In order to convey casualties from the incident to first aid posts or hospitals, a huge expansion of the normal ambulance service was required. This was the emergency or auxiliary ambulance service. Many ambulances and other vehicles were required and at first these were often commercial vehicles loaned to the service every night after business hours. There were also ambulance cars – private cars adapted to take a stretcher on the roof, and sitting case cars which could transport casualties able to sit up. Later, specially built or adapted ambulances were used which were generally capable of carrying four stretchers or six sitting case casualties and were usually in the charge of a driver and an assistant who were usually, but not always, both women.

Like the other mobile services, most ambulances and their crews were stationed at depots, although some were attached to ambulance stations or emergency ambulance stations. When not on call to incidents, they might be used to transport ordinary patients – expectant mothers or elderly people – between hospitals and home, or to take children to and from war nurseries.

Early ambulance teams.

Early casualty service workers, October 1939. (Kent Messenger Group Newspapers)

Kath Barber drove an ARP ambulance in Exeter:

I joined the ARP in 1938 through the WVS. My family thought it was a good idea – they were elderly and I would be able to serve and provide for them at the same time. I became an ambulance driver. They trained us on old laundry vans. We had to learn to drive wearing a gas mask and all the equipment. They picked up a lot of old cars for about £25 each to use as ambulance cars – they just put on a canvas top and stencilled on the letters ARP. I drove an Austin Seven. The Civil Defence transport was based in the bus depot.

In Shakespeare Road the Social Centre, as I suppose it would now be classified, was no. 4 First Aid Post, with Wardens' Posts dotted around on various street corners. As a Civil Defence ambulance driver I spent nights at the post, going in turn to the other first aid posts in other parts of Exeter. I was one of the full-time drivers earning £2 a week – there were many part-time, unpaid drivers who worked on a rota – there were about six or seven ambulances in Exeter. The hours of duty seemed not to matter – we just knew it was work sometimes and a lot of hanging about. Our time was filled in with many activities for which the ambulances could be used, such as billeting evacuees, delivery of blankets and stores to the rest centres, and sometimes patrols from the hospitals in the city.

Our ambulance crew, for a short while, sported a goat mascot, which belonged to Dr Tracey, the captain of our post. Mrs Padbury, our sergeant, billeted it but never paraded it, although it was seen walking in the High Street. Another animal on service was our dog, Teddy, who, if he got the chance of a lift on an ambulance, sat in the seat with a service cap on. Neither animal was on pay-roll.

Training for ambulance staff included first aid and anti-gas, plus maintenance of vehicles and, for drivers, driving in the blackout. Attendants were responsible for equipment, which included stretchers, blankets and first aid equipment, including sandbags, which were used to keep a broken limb immobile during transport.

Tim Clarke drove an ambulance in Liverpool:

As a telephone engineer, I drove a little green van during the daytime and when the blitzes started I volunteered to drive an ambulance at night. My partner on the ambulances was my father's chauffeur (Dad was a

Ambulance service worker. This very clearly shows the CD breast badge, and the smaller version on the ski-cap. This replaced the ARP silver badge.

doctor); unfortunately he was killed on duty at Mill Road Hospital when it was bombed. Luckily for me, I was off sick that night but a few nights later a land-mine was dropped on the massive underground air raid shelter under the Durning Road College, which was only a few yards from our house. I had called home with my ambulance during a lull in the raid, and Dad and I were just coming up from our own cellar air raid shelter when the land-mine exploded. We were both thrown back down the stairs, and when we recovered both of us rushed to help at the college. It was one of the worst incidents of the war, with several hundred people killed and many more buried under the rubble. Many of the families had been in another shelter which was damaged and were told to move to this one by the ARP wardens. Dad stayed down in the depths for many hours tending to the wounded, and when he pronounced them fit to move I, and the other ambulance drivers, drove them to hospital.

The ambulances were generally vehicles like bread vans and such which, because of the shortage of petrol were not required by their owners. The only uniform was a tin hat and an armband with 'AMBULANCE' painted on them. The chief ambulance driver of the group, who spent most of his time at the base, i.e. Mill Road Hospital in our case, wore a white tin hat, the rest of us, black. For large incidents, the chief would appear on site, but generally we would be sent to a bomb site and the ARP wardens there would direct casualties to our ambulances and we would take them to hospital. There were no walkie-talkies so if one hospital had no more room, we would just try driving round to the next one.

Training was fairly basic; usually when we were on duty at the hospital and no alerts on we had talks by the chief, or any nurse or doctor he could find, and we practised applying splints, bandaging or other first aid techniques.

The ambulance service came under the immediate control of the ambulance staff officer who was on the staff of the Medical Officer of Health.

Emergency Mortuaries and Stretcher Parties

One of the least known ARP services, the emergency mortuary service, was set up to handle the vast number of bodies expected as the result of air raids. In each area a series of emergency mortuaries were set up in commandeered premises, suitably equipped, and staffed by volunteers, usually members of cemetery staff or local undertakers. Facilities included equipment for decontaminating bodies exposed to poison gas. Other buildings were earmarked for temporary use, should an emergency arise.

Another of the lesser known casualty services was the stretcher bearers. Unlike the London service – which was another name for first aid parties – these worked exclusively from hospitals, and were made up entirely of volunteers. They unloaded casualties from trains or road convoys and carried them to their wards in the hospital.

CHAPTER 9
Engineer Services I: Gas

Deaths by poison gas made up only a tiny proportion of the total fatalities of the First World War, but gas seized the public imagination; no other weapon was viewed with anything like the terror of aircraft dropping poison gas on an unprotected civilian population, so graphically illustrated in the opening scenes of the 1936 film, *Things to Come*.

In 1925 the Geneva Gas Protocol had been drawn up; this was an agreement banning the first use of gas and was signed by most European countries. In September 1939, as peace ran out, Britain, France and Germany renewed the agreement. In spite of this, much early ARP work was concerned with anti-gas measures; fitting gas masks and instructing householders on such matters as how

Lewisham stretcher party working in anti-gas suits. All CD services had to be able to continue working under gas attack. (Lewisham Local Studies)

to create a gas-proof room in their home. Indeed, the first four ARP handbooks were all primarily concerned with anti-gas measures. Public anxiety increased early in 1936 when press reports began to circulate about the use of mustard gas by the Italian forces in Abyssinia, and cinema newsreels of bombing in Manchuria and Spain only served to heighten this anxiety.

When war did break out, public concern over the possible use of gas against civilians by German aircraft reached its height. As time wore on and gas raids failed to materialise, many of those who had predicted huge casualty lists began to be equally sure that the threat had been vastly overrated. As a result, the habit of carrying gas masks diminished considerably among the general public. The Government, however, continued throughout the war to view poison gas as a threat, repeatedly exhorting the public through poster campaigns to 'carry your gas mask'. In a broadcast on 28 March 1941, Herbert Morrison, Minister of Home Security, warned that '. . . the increased threat of direct attack on this country which the present season brings, involves an increased threat of gas attack.

If the enemy believes it to be to his military advantage to use gas, either in connection with military operations or against the civil population, he will use it – make no doubt of that. Neutral observers, who should be in a good position to form an opinion, have publicly said that Germany is making active preparations to use gas. Whether this is so I cannot say. What I can say is that it is absolutely essential for us to be prepared.

Remember that against a defenceless or ill-prepared population the gas weapon may be deadly – it may even be decisive. But against a well-prepared population which knows what to do and does it, gas can be rendered little more than a serious nuisance. One of the likeliest reasons for the enemy to use gas would be because he might regard it as his last hope of doing what he has tried without any success to do in many other ways – stampeding our civil population and causing it to panic. You can arm yourselves, body and mind, securely against it.'

Later, there was much concern that Germany would use gas against the Russians, or as a last-ditch resort when defeat loomed. A Civil Defence bulletin issued as late as April 1944 reminded wardens to carry their gas rattles with them on patrol for just such an eventuality.

While anti-gas training was an integral part of the syllabus for all ARP volunteers, there were several arms of the ARP services directly concerned with anti-gas measures.

The Decontamination Service

In the First World War, airborne gases, being subject to the whims of the wind, had caused almost as many difficulties for those releasing them as for those 'on the receiving end'. By 1939 it was thought that any gas bombs dropped by aircraft would most likely be of the persistent type; that is to say, they would be in the form of a liquid or jelly, which would evaporate giving off gas.

The primary function of the decontamination service was the decontamination of roads, buildings and materials, including vehicles, from persistent gases, normally by washing away the liquid with a neutralising agent, usually bleach

Street decontamination squad on an exercise. (Kent Messenger Group Newspapers)

powder. It was their foreman's duty to issue a clearance certificate to the incident officer when roads in the area had been made safe for use. Decontamination of people was normally carried out as part of the first aid or casualty process. Later, members of the decontamination service were trained in rescue techniques, and were used to reinforce or relieve the rescue parties.

Decontamination squads consisted of six men, including a driver and a foreman, and were usually stationed at a specialist depot, which had facilities for the decontamination of the squad, their clothing and equipment after exposure. Depots were set up in a ratio of about six depots for every 100,000 of population, and there were usually two squads per depot. The work of decontamination of roads was closely allied to street cleaning, and the personnel of the decontamination squads were usually drawn from this service. The work entailed hard physical labour in heavy decontamination suits, so applicants had to be in good shape physically, as well as intensively trained. Even so, they could only work for at most three hours a day in such conditions.

Each member of the squad was issued with two protective suits, and two suits of special underwear. There was some debate as to when this should be put on; it was recommended that where there were two or more squads operating from the same depot, 'they should be divided into first duty squad, second duty squad, and so on. First duty squad should be in a position to proceed on call at short notice – i.e. changed into special underclothing and socks. Rest of anti-gas gear handy. Next squad to assume same position in readiness when first squad are called out.' Squad equipment included buckets, spades, picks and hoses, plus supplies of bleaching powder and bins for contaminated tools and clothing.

Hull gas exercise. The contaminated area around a gas bomb crater is roped off and signs posted, in line with official procedure. (Hull Central Library)

At first, control of the local decontamination service rested with the Borough Engineer as 'head of the decontamination, rescue, and demolition services', through a superintendent in charge of decontamination. Later, the services separated and the decontamination service had its own head, often the local Chief Public Health Inspector, or Borough Surveyor.

Cleansing Stations

The casualty service was generally responsible for cleansing people exposed to poison gas, whether civil defenders or private citizens. To this end, most first aid posts and hospitals had special sections and specially trained staff to deal with such emergencies. Such treatment was usually in the form of showers. There were also mobile units comprising specially converted vans and lorries.

Eventually the Housewives' Section of the WVS provided facilities for cleansing in most streets, doing away with the need for many of these measures.

Decontamination of Clothing

Another form of decontamination was that of clothing, especially gasproof suits. Most of the civil defence services were expected to be able to carry on their work during and immediately after poison gas attacks, and so were issued 'gasproof suits' to work in. Most, like the wardens, were not expected to work in exposed conditions for long; these people were issued with 'light' gasproof suits. Those –

By the simple addition of a board marked 'Decontamination Squad', this soft drinks lorry has been miraculously transformed. In the early days most ARP transport was borrowed from local firms.

mainly decontamination squads – who were to work for longer periods in exposed conditions, were issued with 'heavy' suits consisting of oilskin jacket, trousers, hood, and gloves, as well as gumboots, helmet and general service gas mask (as issued to the armed forces).

The work of decontaminating these suits after exposure to gas was mainly a matter of boiling the clothing for varying periods according to the texture of their material, so the obvious answer was to use existing laundries, usually those based in hospitals, or commercial laundries. At first, it was thought that the work would be carried out by members of the decontamination squads, but it was seen that this could cause undue strain on the service. In 1941 it was decided that part-time volunteers would be recruited to carry out the task, having first attended a short training course.

The decontamination of civilian clothing was the responsibility of the inspector i/c collection and decontamination of civilian clothing, who was on the staff of the Medical Officer of Health, the service being the responsibility of the Ministry of Health.

Food Decontamination

Food treatment squads were set up to examine, treat or destroy foodstuffs stored in places such as shops or warehouses exposed to gas attack, or affected by burning, exposure to smoke or similar hazards. Food treatment squads were generally made up of workers from the catering industry, usually under the control of the senior sanitary inspector, who was the food decontamination officer, responsible for training. While not members of the ARP general services as such, it was decided in 1941 that members of food treatment squads were eligible for the ARP badge if they had taken the full course of anti-gas training plus the special course in food treatment, and had enrolled as supplementary members of the decontamination service. They were not generally issued with a uniform but those eligible for the badge were entitled to wear the Civil Defence armband while on duty.

Food decontamination officers, leaders and members of treatment squads were distinguished by helmets in different colours bearing the words DC FOOD, as opposed to Public Analysts and appointed chemists who wore yellow helmets marked FOOD ANAL in black!

Gas Identification Service

There was not just one, but a whole catalogue of gases that could be used against the population, and measures against each type varied, so it was vital that, if gas were used, it was quickly and correctly identified. Early in 1937, the Home Office ran two courses for 'gas detectors'; these were people with a scientific background who would form the basis of the gas detection service. The course covered the types of gases most likely to be used in a future conflict, how they could be identified, and what could be done to neutralise or combat them.

In a circular dated 21 September 1939, local authorities were informed that anti-gas services were to be augmented by the creation of a senior gas advisor in every region, who were to be 'persons of high professional standing' in the chemical world. In addition, 1,400 gas identification officers (GIOs), were to be appointed from science teachers in colleges or secondary schools, pharmacists, and so on. GIOs were to be part-time, unpaid volunteers, and were provided on the basis of approximately 3 per 100,000 population. In December the ARP department issued another circular giving details of the equipment to be issued to GIOs and a list of the senior gas advisers.

The Civil Defence gas identification service, as it came to be known, usually came under the local authority's public health department. A senior gas identification officer, often the local chief sanitary inspector, was at its head. In the first instance, gas identification was made by wardens. The GIO and his assistants – usually two – confirmed this identification, gave advice on the extent of its danger and the precautions necessary, and sent a report to control. As with most other experts, their position was advisory – they had no authority over members of the other services.

Large factories had to have their own 'industrial gas identification officer', whose main tasks were to send reports of gas raids on their factory to the report

Decontamination team in heavy anti-gas suits decontaminate a lorry in an exercise using their main equipment of sprays and brushes.

centre and to ensure that the factory could resume work as soon as possible after such an attack. These IGIOs were not enrolled members of the GIO service but were invited to take part in local discussion groups, set up for GIOs. Local authorities could call on them as reinforcements if a widespread gas attack were to take place in their area, but even with their help it was almost certain that under a mass attack the GIOs would have been overwhelmed. Consequently apparatus was devised whose use required far less knowledge and skill than that of the GIO. Called the pocket detector apparatus, it indicated whether an area had to be evacuated and whether CD services needed to wear anti-gas suits. The apparatus consisted of a box, small enough to be carried in the pocket, and a pump contained in a holster, which could be attached to a belt. The box contained a chart, a supply of test papers, glass tubes of test solution, instructions and report forms. It was issued from early 1944, following a circular on its use published in January that year. Training in its use, given mainly to wardens by GIOs, was rushed through.

CHAPTER 10
Engineer Services II: Rescue

Parties trained to rescue survivors from damaged buildings were among the services first described in the original ARP circular of July 1935. The rescue service's main purpose was primarily the extrication of people trapped in bombed buildings, but they were also trained to render first aid and to recover the dead. The task could be huge; on the morning following 'Black Saturday', a police constable, when asked about deaths in his area, replied; 'We've given up digging for the dead. We're still rescuing the living.'

Rescue parties went through several changes in role, as can be seen from their changing titles. At first they were called, 'rescue, repair and demolition parties', and their job included taking the necessary steps for the temporary support or demolition of damaged structures. Later, this was deemed a waste of time for such specialists, and they were not normally required to carry out substantial demolition or shoring, unless there was an immediate risk of collapse which might endanger life, obstruct traffic or hinder the work of the ARP services. They were now called 'rescue parties' and the work of demolishing and shoring up damaged buildings. was done by separate demolition and repair parties, made up of council workmen.

While many of their members had experience in the building trade, it was imperative that they all, from the head of service down, received specialist training in rescue work. Much of their training was based on the lessons learnt from earthquakes: 'Experience shows that there are a number of places in demolished houses where search has proved fruitful: (1) Specially constructed air-raid shelters inside or outside the building. (2) Spaces under staircases. (3) Basements, cellars, coal holes, etc. (4) Places near fireplaces and chimney breasts. (5) Voids and spaces under floors which have not entirely collapsed. (6) Rooms which have not been entirely demolished, but from which exit is barred by debris.'

All members of rescue parties were taught to cut off supplies of gas, water and electricity from damaged buildings. The gas and electricity were as much a danger to the rescuers as those being rescued; the water could be a serious danger to people who were trapped. It was not uncommon for rescue teams to spend hours digging out survivors trapped in a cellar, only to find that the victims had drowned. Paradoxically, the gas mask was of no use against coal gas, the domestic gas used at that time. For this reason, many members of the rescue service were trained in resuscitation, and from 1941 were entitled to wear the badge of the Royal Life Saving Society. To overcome the dangers of coal gas, the remote breathing apparatus was developed. This was basically a general service gas mask with a long hose connected

Gosport rescue squad. This is a standard ten-man rescue squad with their lorry and equipment. Second from right is Mr C.W. Davis.

to it, down which fresh air could be breathed. Every member of the rescue parties had to be trained in its use and by 1942 all members of the rescue service were also trained in first aid. Other training included the use of the stirrup pump, carried by all parties, to put out small fires or to tackle incendiaries. Several regions set up specialist rescue training schools, and in 1944 a national Civil Defence Rescue School was opened in Sutton Coldfield, primarily to train party leaders and local instructors.

At first the standard rescue party was of ten men, including a leader and a driver. They were divided into two categories according to the type of equipment they used: class A parties operated in areas where major incidents involving large buildings might require heavy or specialised equipment; class B parties were more likely to face smaller, isolated incidents. The two types of party were usually classed as heavy and light parties by their use of heavy or light equipment.

Heavy parties were used where there had been extensive damage and collapse of structures requiring a great deal of excavation, perhaps including the use of jacks, blocks and tackles; there was often a specialist in the use of oxyacetylene cutting equipment. The heavy rescue service in most cities also had a number of cranes which could be called out. Searchlights were also available to light up incidents at night, though obviously not during alerts. Late in the war, specially trained dogs began to be used to sniff out buried casualties; some dogs and their handlers were 'loaned out' by the RAF, although there were some dog teams which were part of the Civil Defence services, especially in London. Light parties were used where damage was less extensive, and had a high proportion of first aid experts.

Both sorts of parties, with their equipment and transport, were normally based at depots where at least two parties would be stationed in shifts, so that one party was always on call. Transport for heavy parties would be a large lorry to carry the party and its equipment, but for light parties it might be a van, or even a two-wheeled hand-cart.

It was the driver's job to keep the vehicle maintained and see that all the equipment was properly stowed: it was vital that all equipment could be found immediately, even in the dark. As the team's storekeeper, he was responsible for the upkeep of all equipment and ensuring that none was left behind at the incident. It was recommended that there be three or four rescue parties for every 100,000 population, with one heavy to every four or five light parties; however, all urban areas needed at least one heavy party.

Locally, control of the rescue service rested with a local authority officer, usually called the head of the rescue service, who was often the Borough Engineer or Surveyor. It was their job to oversee the organisation and administration of the rescue service and its personnel, with responsibility for such things as equipment

Light rescue depot, May 1943. The most interesting part of this photograph is the background – the officer wearing collar tabs (centre) is a Regional Officer. The four rescue workers lined up on the right clearly show the profile of the average CD worker, too old for the forces, and, as the farthest, portly old gentleman shows, not always very fit. (Lewisham Local Studies)

and training. During alerts, the head of the rescue service, or his deputy, would normally be found at the Control Centre, ready to call out parties directly from their depots.

Each party was under a leader or foreman. He and three other members of the party would be skilled tradesmen, usually a bricklayer, a plumber and a carpenter, recruited from the building trade, and as such paid more than the ordinary rescue worker. In a major incident where several parties were involved, the first party leader to arrive took control of the rescue services on the spot – all party leaders would have a deputy, who could take over if necessary. The head of service might decide that the incident required a senior officer on site to take charge; this would

Rescue workers playing netball. Organised sports formed a part of every CD worker's training.

usually be a rescue party supervisor, often a member of the Borough Engineer's staff or a local master builder, trained in rescue techniques and control. It would be his job to direct the various parties, through their party leaders – individual party members were trained to take directions only from their own party leader or deputy.

At the end of 1941, the London stretcher parties were re-formed into light rescue parties. These were still five-strong, including a leader and driver, and just over a year later, in January 1943, the rest of the country followed suit with the first aid parties being amalgamated into the rescue service as light rescue parties. One major problem was that rescue parties consisted of men only, whereas in some areas women made up some of the first aid parties. Women members of first aid parties, it was decided, could be transferred to other Civil Defence services, such as the wardens' or ambulance services, which already had women members. Towards the end of that year it was agreed that all rescue parties should consist of seven men including driver and leader, except in London where the size of party remained at five for light and ten for heavy.

Many rescues would carry on for hours, if not days, continuing throughout alerts and actual bombing. It soon became apparent that rescue parties had to be appropriately dressed, and it is no coincidence that rescue workers were the first to be issued with a proper uniform – although many continued to use the bluette overalls. Rescue teams photographed during raids (or official exercises) are usually wearing helmets, but photographs taken at other times almost invariably show them wearing the flat caps and trilby hats worn by all workmen of the period. Special equipment issued to individual rescue party members included protective gloves, a clasp knife, a hand-lamp and often a hand-axe, sometimes carried in a white sling-type carrier or, if using a fireman's axe, in a fire service webbing belt.

Continuing to dig among the dangers of collapsing buildings, possible explosions of gas, or even bombs, required great courage, and it is not surprising that many rescue workers were decorated for bravery. The *Lewisham Borough News* of 17 June 1941 reported on the award of the George Medal to George Groom, a member of the Deptford Rescue Service:

'It happened back in September', Mr Groom said, 'when we were first experiencing the German night attacks. Bombs were dropped at Deptford and a number of shops had been hit.' The report continues: 'The Rescue Squad to which Groom belongs was called out on this incident. When they arrived they found that the bomb had also burst a water main and the cellars under the shop, where a number of people were sheltering, were flooding rapidly. Fortunately the debris was being held up by some furniture.

'Without any heed to the great danger, Groom managed to crawl through part of the debris. It was in a slippery condition and many times he found himself up to his neck and once or twice was under water.

Admiral Evans, one of the two London regional commissioners, inspecting a heavy rescue depot, May 1943. Note the signs on their lorries (at rear), and the special London Rescue Service breast badges. (Lewisham Local Studies)

Hull rescue workers listening at the rubble for sounds of survivors, actually a very effective practice. (Hull Central Library)

'Meanwhile more bombs were falling close by and the vibration was causing the debris to slip all the time. The AFS aided the rescue work by keeping the water under control.

'After four hours of toil and exhaustion they managed to rescue three people. Fortunately, in two cases, their efforts had not been in vain, for a father and a daughter were rescued alive. . . .

'When the gang first arrived on the scene,' said Mr Groom, 'there was already a large number of people attacking the debris from the top. My gang approached from another angle. It was all very confusing – stairs were smashed in, and we had to go through the basement of an adjoining shop. All the time the water was rising rapidly and we tried many ways to get there.

'There was no time to think about Jerry, although the whole area was lit up with burning incendiaries and fires. We had to concentrate on getting the people out.'

'On another occasion a large Deptford hall had been hit and once again George Groom and his rescue squad were called upon to effect rescue work.

'The incident happened during a daylight raid and many casualties were involved. The hall had been hit in two or three places. People had crowded into an adjoining room, and this was one of the places that had been hit. A concrete floor above the room collapsed on the occupants.

'We managed to get a few people out when we arrived there,' Mr Groom told me. 'The water was pouring in on us all the time as the firemen were using their hoses to put out a fire on top of the building.

'The water caused a lot of brickwork to come down on us, thus hampering the rescue work. This was an even worse job than the last one.'

'During the course of rescue work Groom was trapped, but was able to get free again. After two hours of being soaked to the skin and in a shivering condition he was forced to retire and was taken to hospital. During the time he was on the scene, fourteen people had been rescued.'

CHAPTER 11

Police

During 1938 it was accepted that, in a future war, the duties of the police would increase so enormously that the pre-war forces would be unable to cope. The numbers of police had to be trebled. This was accomplished using three sources; the First Police Reserve, comprising police pensioners, the Second Reserve, of Special Constables, part-time and unpaid, and the Third Reserve, which was a War Reserve – a full-time force who were signed up for war service only. At first all police were regarded as being in reserved occupations, later the increasing demands on personnel meant that the regular police were 'de-reserved' up to the age of thirty, and war reservists up to thirty-three; leaving even more work for the 'specials'.

Women's Auxiliary Police Constable Mary Dunning, Birmingham City Police. Her light blue WAPC shoulder flash is just visible.

Jack Withersby joined the War Reserve Police in London; 'About May 1939, with a friend, I answered the call for volunteers and joined the War Reserve Police at Brockley nick, attending weekly lectures. On 2nd September I was called up and after being sworn in, was sent to Catford to be kitted out. This consisted of a steel helmet, whistle, notebook and truncheon (a piece of wood like a thick broom handle with a piece of cord for a wrist strap), then back to Brockley for a service-type respirator and gas protective clothing. Uniforms came later.

I did a few weeks in ordinary beat duty at Brockley, then was transferred to a 'group'

Four Maidstone WAPCs, February 1942. Each force had its own uniforms and insignia. Compare this with the picture opposite. (Kent Messenger Group Newspapers)

station at Ivydale Road School – it was there on the beat that I was able to visit the pumping station officially at the reservoir at Nunhead. It was a recognised call to check that everything was in order, also to call on Wardens' Posts and First Aid Posts along the beat.

Volunteers were called for transfer to the sub-divisional station at Lewisham to go on 'divisional transport'. I was accepted after passing a driving test. On day-duty it was mainly on the beat, on night-duty, driving cars and vans on any occasion required, such as picking up drunks, patrolling with an inspector, attending at bomb incidents or helping evacuate people and roping off areas where unexploded bombs had fallen – in fact, anything where transport was needed.

Another source of personnel was the Women's Auxiliary Police Corps. Originally the idea was to recruit women for clerical work only in Divisional and Sub-Divisional offices. WAPCs also helped in administrative work and as drivers. Their numbers were small, at their height less than 10,000 – some forces employed no women at all.

In the run-up to the war police stations were strengthened to make them more bomb-resistant, either structurally or by the use of sandbags. In many areas, reserve stations were set up; suitable buildings were converted and equipped so that, if the main station were to be put out of action, the reserve station could be brought into play.

Maidstone PC on point duty, wearing gas mask and white gauntlets for extra visibility in the blackout. (Kent Messenger Group Newspapers)

Outside London, the police were usually in charge of incidents; Hugh Learmont was a regular in Liverpool: 'The Chief Constable, Herbert Winstanley, was responsible for the overall operational control of ARP/Civil Defence. There was also a Chief Air Raid Warden named Robert Blues. After an air raid warden reported unexploded bombs in various places, the divisional inspector had to make an inspection to decide what evacuations were necessary. I often drove him to the site, but the bombs fortunately never went off when we were there. Two of my colleagues were not so lucky; they went to a school one night to investigate a report of a parachute mine having landed. As they entered the building it exploded – they were never found. Another constable in my department, when off duty, was standing at his garden gate when a parachute mine fell on his house and blew it to bits. Incredibly he was not injured – lucky man!'

The blackout was one of the biggest headaches for the police. Wardens were responsible for public compliance but were not able to deal directly with those who refused to comply – they had to report them to the police. This of course related to vehicles as well as private and commercial premises. The blackout provided the perfect cover for criminal activities of all sorts, and it also made the roads hazardous. Jack Withersby recalls: 'The funniest thing I can remember was on point duty outside Lewisham Town Hall one night in the blackout. We used a cycle lamp with red glass to wave at the drivers – which was all right on moonlit

Dover policeman arrests German airman. Bailed-out enemy airmen were usually handed over to the local police until the military arrived.

nights, but a bit hairy on dark ones. At this point there was an island in the road with underground toilets; I had signalled the traffic to come on and a man in an Austin 10 came towards me but didn't see the island. He charged up on it and went down the steps of the ladies' but managed to stop with the rear wheels on pavement level. I had to jump very smartly out of the way – luckily I was just going off duty and 'didn't see anything' – I wonder how he opened the door to get out!

Another interesting thing about night driving which I should mention is the lighting situation on all vehicles and traffic lights. All lenses on traffic lights were permanently covered with a black metal plate pierced by a cross (+), making them very difficult to see in daylight. Car headlights had to be covered the same way except for a horizontal slot three-quarters of an inch wide, and sidelights painted black leaving only a light of 1-inch diameter. Cycle lamps were hooded – it was certainly no picnic being on the road in the blackout.'

The vast increase in juvenile crime, often due to fathers being away for long periods with the forces, and mothers working long hours in the factories, caused a great deal of concern. The stresses of war led to a sharp drop in public morality – shelters were frequently used by courting couples, and prostitution became blatant, especially with the arrival of the US troops, with 'ladies' touting for business in the larger public shelters, and often carrying it out in the smaller abandoned surface shelters. Patrols were increased to cope with all this.

Jack Withersby recalled:

Most people who have watched police series on television or read crime books will have heard the terms 'my patch' or 'my manor', but I can only say that in my two and a half years of mixing with 'regulars' I never heard the expression – it was always 'my ground'.

In pre-war days they were fairly large and each man carried a beat book. The beat would be worked in four separate ways, A, B, C or D, and the Duty Sergeant decided at parade time how it would be worked. The reason for this is obvious. With the large number of men available in wartime the beats were carved up into very small areas to give the ground more coverage but Crime Patrols were not altered and were always covered by the regulars. These patrols were always in vulnerable shopping areas.

Other new tasks for the police included dealing with incendiaries, gas, unexploded bombs, crashed aircraft, loose barrage balloons, national registration, enemy aliens and drunken servicemen. Then there were lesser-known restrictions: balloons and kites were not to be flown; fireworks were banned, likewise noises such as bells, sirens and factory hooters. The size of crowds had to be limited and there were restrictions on using cameras. The CID had to be ready to take on looting, sabotage and black marketeering, although, as it transpired, cases of sabotage were almost non-existent. Special Branch kept a close eye on potential fifth columnists and spies.

When, in May 1940, the Local Defence Volunteers (later the Home Guard) was formed, volunteers were told to register at their local police station. The scale of the task was enormous. To arm this new force, the government appealed to the public to hand any weapons in to the police, and so everything from expensive shotguns to Zulu spears poured into police stations. Indeed, there were many calls for the police to be armed, and although this never took place, police units often took part in armed invasion exercises with the Home Guard, and received arms training with them.

Jack Withersby added: 'The Police War Reserve were supposed to have rifle and pistol training. We did – one afternoon we were taken to the police range at Beckenham and given five rounds each on rifle and pistol. With that amount of training I wonder what would have happened had we ever been called on to use guns.'

The police had specific duties at the scene of an incident: cordoning off the area, keeping the roads open for essential traffic, diverting other traffic, setting up parking areas for service vehicles, controlling crowds and preventing looting while police motor-cyclists scouted out and marked diversions. If damaged buildings were considered dangerous, a police officer of the rank of inspector or above could order demolition. If all else was under control, constables would help with the rescue work. To this end, all police were trained in first aid, fire-fighting, rescue and anti-gas work. After the rescue work was done, it was the work of the police to compile casualty lists of the dead and injured, and, of course, to inform relatives. Other forms of specific training included incident control and bomb reconnaissance.

Hugh Learmont recalls:

I joined the Liverpool City Police in 1929, and in 1932 transferred into the Motor Transport Department as an ambulance driver, police van driver, and in the pre-war years, a road patrol driver. In those days the police ran the ambulance and fire services.

In 1938, local ARP training commenced in this city under the supervision of the City Police. All the force had to take part. Training took place at the old police training department, known as Everton Terrace. It was in two parts: gas drill, and fire-fighting methods. For the first you were dressed in overalls, rubber boots, gauntlets, service respirator and steel helmet. It was very cumbersome. The test in-volved exposure to phosgene gas (phosgene was a deadly,

Metropolitan mounted police in wartime order.

non-persistent, choking gas). For this purpose, a large Commer van was fitted with an airtight door at the rear with a ramp at the back. The Instructor lit a lamp which heated a capsule. This filled the interior with a cloud of poison gas. The idea was to show that you could still breathe in the event of the possible gas attack made by the enemy. This so-called Gas Van was used on many occasions to train service and civilian ARP members.

The fire-fighting drill consisted of creating a blaze in a corrugated iron shed in the yard. You crawled into it with a stirrup pump to try to extinguish the fire. Later on, when civilian fire watchers were recruited, lectures on incendiary bombs were held in the city centre.

Local stations had to submit regular reports, known as situation reports, to divisional HQ, and thence to the Regional Commissioner. Possible disruption of communications by bombs presented a problem. As with ARP control centres, extra telephone lines were installed, as were extra teleprinter lines. But although this went some way to alleviate the problem, there was still a possibility that a few unfortunately placed bombs would cause a breakdown. Most forces therefore had a back-up wireless system which had the added benefit that, should a station be put out of order – and several were indeed

Tin-helmeted WPC helping with evacuees.

hit, and some destroyed – emergency premises could be put into immediate contact with headquarters.

Jack Withersby remembered:

All Divisional stations were in direct radio contact with Scotland Yard and every sub-divisional station had a radio receiver and transmitter. When a raid was coming, a radio call went out to divisional stations: Air Raid Message Yellow. This would be passed on to sub-divisional stations by telephone with the added instruction 'switch to radio'. Local stations were then alerted by phone from the 'subs'. The next was Air Raid Message Purple, followed, if necessary, by the Red and 'sound siren'.

At Lewisham on driving duty, I was able to spend a lot of time in the communications room (a converted cell). In here were two lamp-signalling switchboards both with outside lines to two different exchanges (Lee Green and Hither Green) in case of breakdowns or disruptions. They also had direct lines to several surrounding stations and the old blue 'police' street boxes, some with sirens.

Also in the cell was a very large radio about five feet high and two feet wide with banks of valves – and the siren switch. This was a semi-circular iron box with a large handle, held in the 'off' position by a heavy iron-hinged clamp straddling the handle like a fork. This clamp had to be lifted with one hand and the switch moved left or right, to red or green, with the other hand. This was to prevent accidental sounding of the siren. The sounding time was two minutes, and it has been my doubtful pleasure to sound it several times. [In 1938 it had been agreed that the responsibility for sounding the sirens should rest with the police, so many of the sirens were sited on top of police stations or police boxes. At first these were operated individually but, after several false alerts, were connected locally to a master control, usually based in the main police station.]

The transmitter was only used to reply 'OK Radio' followed by the station code during the daily test by Scotland Yard. Sets were switched on at 10 a.m. all over the London area and each station could be heard being called (but not the reply). Being in P Division, we were well down the list.

Two young police auxiliary messengers in Maidstone, March 1942. (Kent Messenger Group Newspapers)

War Reserve PC in early 'uniform' on duty outside No. 10 Downing Street.

In March 1942 an order was made releasing men for war work with a two-hour re-call if necessary, the uniform and equipment being kept at the station – which had to be informed of your address if you went on holiday or away from home overnight.

The police had their own messengers, the Police Auxiliary Messenger Service. Mike Bree joined the PAMS in Penzance: 'When I left school in 1943, waiting to join the Navy, I took a job at the local police station as a police messenger. My tasks were obviously those of station dogsbody or gofer. One of the jobs that fell to my lot, when I was suddenly sent to work with the CID branch, was registering the aliens, which had to be done at intervals.'

CHAPTER 12

Fire

Of the three types of weapon expected to be deployed from the air, gas and high explosives were seen before the war as posing the biggest threat. Incendiaries were regarded very much as a minor danger – fires were expected, but more as a result of high explosive than mass incendiary drops. A large expansion of the existing fire brigades in the form of the Auxiliary Fire Service was considered the appropriate response to this threat.

However, one of the most effective aerial weapons employed by the Luftwaffe in the assault on Britain's cities was the 1 kilo Electron incendiary bomb. Its main advantage was its size – a heavy bomber could carry almost 1,000; the Home Office calculated that a single German bomber could start up to 150 fires spread over three miles. This took into account the high proportion that failed to go off or fell on such 'stoney ground' as roads or wasteland. In the raid on the City of London on 29 December 1940, the Germans claimed to have dropped 100,000 incendiaries – probably a fairly accurate claim. In *It Came to Our Door*, published in 1946, H.P. Twyford described the sound of incendiaries falling: 'I do not think anyone who went through those raids will ever forget the very distinctive sound they made as they fell in their thousands. The nearest description was to that of dried leaves being rustled along the pavements and gutters by a high wind in the darkness.'

The following description, by a bus conductress, of an incendiary attack is from *Hell's Kitchen, 1940*:

. . . there was a great hissing sound and the place became a mass of light. The bus was brought to a standstill, and the lady passenger asked 'What shall we do, miss?'

I replied, 'If anything comes down near us lie flat on the floor of the bus.'

Meanwhile I pulled up the back seats and took out the sandbags, which we carried, and went to hand some of them to the driver. But he had got down from his seat and had just come to the back of the bus.

Just at that moment more incendiaries fell, and one fell on the back of the bus, so I kicked it straight off, and it exploded into about a hundred bright lights. I dropped a sandbag on it.

We saw some incendiaries burning on the lawn of a house where we had pulled up, so, as the German 'plane was still overhead, we found a piece of old slate and dug up some earth with it and covered the flames.

" Come on, Andra, we can go hame !   The place is burnt doon ! '

By courtesy of the " Weekly News

Fire watchers. A common joke of the period was that fire watchers spent all their time sleeping –
e.g. 'I slept as soundly as a fire watcher last night!'

The AFS soon drove up, and I directed them to a house where an incendiary had gone through the roof. We had tried to get into the house ourselves, but could not do so as it was locked and the people were away.

We helped to fill sandbags from a sand heap and some soldiers came and lent a hand. We covered some other incendiaries with the lid of a dustbin, which we borrowed from someone's backyard.

The whole affair was over in 20 minutes, and the bus proceeded once more on its way.

As this account shows, the small size of the Electron meant that it could be fairly easily extinguished if dealt with quickly, but left alone could soon develop into a major fire. It was the huge numbers of these incendiaries dropped that made them so effective. Even taking the expansion of the fire brigades into account, a large raid could cause far too many fires to be dealt with by them alone. At first it was thought that fighting incendiaries would be part of the task of the wardens, although it soon became obvious that the wardens were already overstretched. Then it was considered that householders should bear the brunt in residential areas, using the stirrup pump, specially designed for the task, and the Redhill scoop, a sort of long-handled shovel. To supplement this, it became common to leave sandbags on the side of the road, or by telegraph poles. These were to be used against incendiaries by anyone passing, but as dogs will be dogs, war or not, such supplies often became most unsavoury.

A system of fire watchers in industrial premises was added to this. Members of staff would keep a watch at night on a rota for falling incendiaries and would contact the fire service before they took hold.

Len Wright was a Fire Watcher in London:

At the beginning of the war I worked for the Home Office. I regularly did a stint as a fire watcher. The Home Office laid on instruction by the fire brigade; I remember they gave us a hose and told us to direct it into the bottom of a pit – the force of the jet lifted us into the air so the firemen laughed themselves silly. We were given a stirrup pump. I don't recall any other equipment, not even a helmet. Of course, we all had gas masks – everyone had one of those. One went on to the roof of the building and if an incendiary bomb fell, one tried to put it out. If the bombing was too heavy they took us down to the shelters.

I did as many fire watching shifts as I could – we were given one and sixpence subsistence allowance and at that time I was only earning thirty-seven and six a week.

Tim Clarke was a telephone engineer in Liverpool: 'I had to do fire watching at the two buildings which comprised the exchange. One was an old half-timbered building in the valley, and the other was a brand-new, red-brick structure about half a mile up a very steep hill. It had a flat roof, and gave wonderful views of the fires raging in Liverpool. The building was empty as all the equipment had been taken out to replace bomb-damaged telephone equipment in Lancaster House, Liverpool's main trunk exchange. As a fire-watcher the main equipment was buckets full of sand, and a stirrup pump and bucket of water. And a whistle!'

The Auxiliary Fire Service

The Home Office fire advisor pointed out as early as 1932 that a great expansion of the existing fire brigades would be needed in a future war. In January 1938 the government urged local authorities to set up an Emergency Fire Brigade Organisation, including Auxiliary Fire Stations and the recruitment and training of personnel. In July 1938 the Fire Brigades Act gave local authorities two years to bring their brigades up to strength and expansion was pushed ahead. This was often done through local advertising campaigns.

George Grigs was involved in one such:

Before the war, and for some time after it, I worked for a well-known advertising agency in St Martin's Lane – the London Press Exchange, more commonly known as the LPE. I was in the Art Section, mainly concerned with the visual work. Around the early part of 1939 we were asked by the London

County Council to prepare an advertising campaign for recruitment to the AFS. Ward Burton (the account executive for my group) and a copywriter and I discussed the briefing. After I had prepared one or two very rough 'roughs', a more finished presentation was agreed upon, and it was in this form that the campaign was presented by Ward Burton and me to Herbert Morrison at the County Hall. One other man was present on the LCC side, but I've no idea who he was; in any case, Morrison was the boss. After some discussion the campaign was agreed upon, and all concerned set to work on it.

Perhaps impressed by my own work I volunteered myself somewhere around June or July of that year at Shaftesbury Avenue (station number 72Y).

The results were varied – in the week following the Munich Crisis, the *Daily Herald* reported that 'Since last Saturday there have been 7,568 applications for enrolment in London's Auxiliary Fire Service. In addition 4,000 people applied by newspaper coupons during the last two days.' On the other hand Councillor James McInnes, of Glasgow, writing in 1944, recalled: 'In those days Auxiliary Firemen were paid £1 on enrolling but I prefer to forget the multitude who, after receiving the £1, were posted as "missing"!'

By the end of 1938, just over 80,000 had enrolled, less than half the number required, although soon after the outbreak of war the number was almost up to the full £200,000. Councillor McInnes again: 'With the outbreak of hostilities we were so inundated with recruits that we had to engage five doctors to carry out medical examinations. So heavy did this work become that examinations had to be made every evening and on Sundays at the City Chambers.' Numbers on this scale created other problems; the normal brigade training officers were swamped, and most auxiliaries were trained by serving firemen, whose approach was rarely academic but usually practical. Charlie Wheeler joined the AFS in Liverpool and he recalls that they were issued with the instruction that, as a last resort, 'every man was his own stirrup pump!'

Auxiliary fire stations sprang up in all sorts of buildings, on the principle of dispersal: if a town's fire engines (pumps) were all concentrated in one large station, and that station were hit early in a raid, effectively the whole fire service could be put out of action. Each station had its own beat where fire patrols, under a patrol officer, patrolled at frequent intervals so that delay in attacking fires would be reduced to a minimum – theoretically. In fact, the wardens, and later, the fire guards, proved, on the whole, to be so effective that such patrols became unnecessary.

On the last day of August 1939, with war looming, firemen were issued with tin helmets, red engines were repainted in wartime grey, and AFS personnel were summoned to their stations. Frank Padgham was a member of the AFS in Southsea:

On the afternoon of September 2nd 1939, I received instructions to report to the fire station near the Guildhall. There were several other fellows gathered there and we were all officially enrolled in the new conscript Fire Service and each given some equipment and overalls and a number. We were addressed by

Sergeant Hicks of the City Fire Brigade and told in very plain language (with many expletives) that we were on war service and under orders from the crown. He also said we were to receive £2 18s per week. I and several others were instructed to report at 10 p.m. that night to a large showroom of a car sales building in Clarendon Road, Southsea, and he impressed on us that this was not a request, but an order.

At last the time came for me to go to my appointed place. There, a number of lads were gathering and we were all directed by a police officer to the large showroom upstairs which was empty except for tables and chairs. The police officer then gave us a pep talk and informed us that we were to spend the night there. At 6 the next morning we were to be sent home and were to return without fail at 6 that night, when we would be split up into crews and sent to a new rendezvous.

There were facilities to make tea and we had all brought some sandwiches so we settled down in groups and whiled the hours away chatting to each other, wondering whether at 11 the next morning the PM, who was to make a

AFS crew. Their breast badges identify them as from London, and their helmets and ladders on the pump identify them as from station 42W. On their webbing belts can clearly be seen their axes, hemp lines and hose spanners.

broadcast, would announce that we were actually at war with Germany. The hours passed slowly, and at 6 a.m. on that fateful Sunday we were dismissed and told to report back at 6 that night when we would get our new posting. Once again, the police officer reminded us very forcefully that if any of us failed to report that night we would be in serious trouble.

Six p.m. came round at last and I set off to report as ordered for our new posting. Outside were some vehicles and some of us were told to be ready for our new rendezvous. Off we went and to our utter amazement we pulled up at a private house in Craneswater Avenue. This had been taken over and we were to make this just another temporary station. The large main room was furnished with tables and chairs and we met for the first time a young lady who was to be the telephonist. Waiting to receive us was Mr Bray who had been appointed a Patrol Officer. He straight away began to put us in the picture as to possible action in the future. He told us we were only to be there for about seven days during which time a permanent station was hurriedly being prepared. He reminded us very seriously that we were to be ready for enemy action at any time, which was a sobering thought. How we would have shaped up if air raids had started I don't know as we were at best only very amateur with little training and no experience. Thank goodness many months were to pass and much training done before we actually went into action. Every one of us in the Civil Defence Force so hastily mobilised were determined to do our best but we were so lacking in training and experience. It was a very different story when the Battle of Britain commenced some nine months later.

In the garage adjacent was a lorry to which was attached a Climax Fire Pump and one of our group who happened to be a lorry driver was detailed as the driver.

Mr Bray then left us to our own devices while he went on to do the same with another group of lads some distance away. We began to sort ourselves out for another night's duty and to await the morning when we would be relieved by a new group of lads.

Most AFS crews were issued with trailer pumps. As the name implied, these needed towing, but they were rarely accompanied by towing vehicles. At first saloon cars were purchased for the purpose. Sometimes lorries and vans were borrowed from local firms, sometimes, as in London, taxis were hired for the job. George Grigs said of the London taxis: 'Another memory was being instructed by our "boss", a seasoned fireman named Gravett, to take one of our taxis somewhere to pick something up. None was available, and when I reported this to Gravett, he said very forcibly, "Well – go and get one; commandeer it from the driver." So I walked across to Greek Street, where I spotted a taxi parked outside a café. I went in to ask where the driver was, and as no one knew, simply took ALE 199 back to 72Y, leaving it to the authorities to sort the matter out.'

Gus Capaldi remembers this period: 'I joined the AFS in Glasgow in October 1940. I tried first to join the army, but as Italy had joined in the war against us a few months before they wouldn't have me' [he was of Italian extraction]. 'I didn't pass my driving test at first; the man who tested you was a real barrow boy; he bought up old cars and vans and sold them to the fire brigade. Well, if you wanted him to pass you you had to drop him a fiver. In those days I couldn't afford that, then a pal of mine who had passed said to me, 'You're as good a driver as I am. I'll see my boss, Mr Campbell, he'll be able to help.' Well he did, and so I became a driver; I was at station A4, Kenning Park. I drove all sorts, at first they were just old cars, vans or lorries used to tow the trailer. The trailer pumped up the water into the hoses. When we got to the fire, I had to work the trailer.' Eventually special vans were supplied to tow the trailers.

Slowly things began to take shape. Frank Padgham recalled:

After a whole week of night duty with very little to do, we were delighted to be told that fire stations had been prepared all over the city and these were getting into shape. So at last we moved to a very large, empty garage which had been requisitioned in Granada Road, Southsea, and where we were to commence quite a long stay. When we arrived, together with a number of other lads, we found there were about five fire pumps with private cars to tow them. A kitchen area had been hastily prepared and a control room installed. We were lined up in our new fire station and given a complete run-down of our future. The lads were divided into two sections; one to be on day shift and the other on the night shift. We were to start immediately on twelve-hour shifts while half of the lads were sent home to return for the night shift. We met for the first time our new Patrol Officers and leading firemen and they began to organise us into a proper routine for day and night shifts.

The kitchen area was very limited but reasonably adequate and on our shift, two of the lads volunteered to be caterer/cook. We had to provide our own food and after consultation the caterer fixed what he thought was a reasonable sum of money we each had to pay him every week. He was then sent to various shops near the station to put in a weekly order for provisions.

A time was set for meal breaks, and the remainder of the time we followed a full schedule of drills with the pumps plus cleaning the station and polishing all the brasses on the pumps. Those who were qualified drivers were made pump drivers and in addition to the officer in charge, five lads were appointed leading firemen in charge of a pump.

The first day passed very quickly and we soon got to know each other and during the standby periods we were able to relax in a section partitioned off as a recreation room with the inevitable dart-board and chairs to relax in. No beds were provided at this early stage but it wasn't long before camp beds and deck chairs appeared – we were very near the beach and I'm sure the man who looked after the deck chairs must have wondered when quite a few of his deck chairs suddenly went missing.

As is usual, the lads got themselves into their own little groups according to their temperament but we all settled down into quite a pleasant lifestyle. Card schools soon got under way in our standby patrols and I soon got quite proficient in darts and what the ex-navy lads called 'uckers' – ludo.

One day we were pleased to be told that at last uniforms were to be issued, consisting of a tunic with two rows of silver buttons, and serge trousers. This did a great deal for our morale.

George VI inspects WAFS, October 1940. Note the early bluette uniforms, and the WAFS district officer's hat and epaulette rank badges.

As well as pumps, many brigades possessed fire boats, or fire floats as they were often called. One London fire float, the Massey Shaw, was one of the 'little boats' at Dunkirk, manned by six LFB and six AFS firemen.

There were two Auxiliary Services, the AFS, which was mainly made up of men, with some youths used as messengers, and the WAFS – Women's Auxiliary Fire Service – most of whom worked in control centres and stations as telephonists and clerical workers, in mobile canteens, and as drivers and despatch riders. Eva Tynan was in the Women's Auxiliary Fire Service. She had been a top quality dressmaker but was called up in 1940:

I was made a driver – we were taught to drive all kinds of vehicles. We had to be able to drive them in the blackout without any headlights. We went up to County Hall for our test; I had driven before the war so I passed first time.

It ruined my hands – we had to keep our vehicles clean, get underneath and grease them and so on – and I couldn't go back to dressmaking after the war. My first job was to drive a petrol lorry out to a fire; this was needed to re-fuel the pumps. There were incendiaries dropping all around; I told the DI with me that I was sure we'd all go up in smoke.

I was based at Clapham Old Town. When I first started they weren't ready for us – we had to wear old firemen's uniforms, boots and all, and we were all used to high heels! We were given a bunk bed, but there was no mattress on it –

I had to go home and collect up all the pillows – although we never got a full night's sleep.

We did a bit of everything; sometimes we drove the mobile canteens to a big fire, serving tea and sandwiches to the men there, sometimes we drove staff cars. The firemen weren't used to women working with them and some of them didn't like it. They used to let down the tyres of our staff cars. We had to cook for ourselves, and once, when we were boiling cabbage, one of them put a bar of soap in it; but we forgave them, they worked so hard.

The phoney war and the criticisms of Civil Defence which went with it seemed to apply especially to the AFS: 'Fifty bob a week army dodgers, they called us', one said. Large numbers of volunteers left during the spring and summer of 1940, George Grigs was one of them: 'After a while, and tiring of routine drills and pointless exercises (many in the blackout), but above all as nothing was happening, I left the AFS and joined the army. Later I learned that 72Y had suffered a direct hit, and that many of my old friends had been killed.'

Then the blitz came – Frank Padgham vividly recalls a raid on Portsmouth:

We began to wonder when our turn would come – we didn't have long to wait. On January 10th I was at home on day leave when the sirens sounded and within a few minutes all the lights went out. I got out my cycle to return to the

ME–AFS 72Y assembled on the roof of Peter Street School, Soho, October/November 1939. George Grigs is second row back, third from the left. The three men in the centre of that row are regular LFB men, the outer two recognisable as such by their pork-pie hats; Gravett is the one on the left, the station officer in the centre was called 'Lofty'.

Firemen wearing oxygen apparatus and anti-spark goggles.

station and all the others, my family and several visitors, somehow crowded into our little Anderson shelter. As I pedalled furiously to the fire station I was really scared as bombs and incendiaries were whistling down. When I arrived I was just in time to hear the alarm bell sounding so I donned my fire kit and jumped on a fire engine just as it was leaving.

We had been ordered to report to the Guildhall and we turned down into Palmerston Road. What a shock for us all at what we saw! The whole of the Palmerston Road shops and houses were ablaze and what used to be Handleys (now Debenhams) was a sight I shall never forget. On all floors blood-red flames were pouring out of every window. There did not seem to be anywhere that wasn't on fire. Here a rather amusing thing happened; a special constable flagged us down and asked if we could give him assistance. He pointed to a large house, well alight on the upper floors, and a very elderly lady was standing firm. The policeman said he had been doing his best to get her to come out as the house would very soon be completely in flames. She just folded her arms and said defiantly that she wasn't going to be driven out by that B—— Hitler. We gradually calmed her down and the PC was able to lead her out into the street and we mounted our machine and were off to our appointed reporting place at the Guildhall. There was an amazing sight for the old Guildhall was completely ablaze and flames were coming out of the tower at the top. All around us were fires, all out of control.

We were met by a senior officer who looked distraught – he pointed to a hydrant which was turned fully on and said sadly: 'Sorry lads, there's not a drop of water in the mains round here and there's nothing we can do.' He ordered us to go back, on the way stopping at any of the 5,000 emergency water tanks in the city that were near a fire, and do what we could. We were told later that at its peak that night there were over 2,000 fires and most of the water mains were burst by bombs.

By this time, large numbers of reinforcements were arriving from miles around, many convoys bringing in water tenders, and a water relay was set up from Clarence Pier to the centre of the city. This of course takes quite a time but once installed, it was a great help. However Commercial Road and the dockyard area, as well as the main shopping areas in Southsea were completely destroyed by fire and high explosive bombs. Another area severely damaged was the High Street, Old Portsmouth. There were fires all around the cathedral, but miraculously it escaped damage.

The raid carried on for what seemed like hours and what with the bombs and the anti-aircraft gunfire, the noise was terrific. As we were leaving the Guildhall there was a terrific explosion and we were showered with bricks and dust; we escaped by seconds, but, sad to relate, one of the lads we had been talking to just a few seconds before was killed outright. How fortunate our crew were, we didn't know until later.

NFS trailer crew from Holcombe Fire Station, Chatham. The station was most unusual in that it was entirely run by women. (Kent Messenger Group Newspapers)

We proceeded as ordered and at the next water dam we stopped as it was close to a small terraced house, well alight, and we made every effort to put out the fire – but alas it was too late to save it.

We progressed slowly back to our station with the din overhead going on relentlessly and incendiary bombs falling like rain. Suddenly it became quiet and it was a strange feeling not to hear the incessant noise of exploding bombs and heavy gunfire. The raid was over after about two hours of merciless destruction, but we had only just begun. On arrival back at the station we were sent out again immediately to try our best to deal with a number of fires. We were instructed to go wherever was necessary to deal with any fire that had a water supply nearby and attempt any rescue work, and help folks whose houses were either destroyed or well alight, to places of safety. It

The salvage corps at work rescuing material and goods after a fire. Note the 'S' armbands.

was a heart-rending job as many elderly people were in an awful state and in need of first aid and comfort.

The hours wore on and we had lost all sense of time when a senior officer came in his car and told our crew that reinforcements were now in action and we were relieved; we could have six hours to go home if we wanted, or back to the station, for food and rest. I was amazed to realise that it was midday and that we had been in action for eighteen hours! Fortunately we were working only a short distance from my home so I made my way on foot, wondering if my house was still there and my family safe. What a relief to see Eton Road untouched, although a few yards further on the girls' secondary school was still burning. It wasn't till I got indoors that I realised how hungry and exhausted I was. Anyhow I had six hours to relax – it's marvellous what a hot cup of tea can do.

I tried to relax and, oh so quickly, the time came for me to return to the station. On the roll call parade we were distressed to learn that one of our lads was missing – it was two days later that his body was found under a house that had collapsed on him.

The National Fire Service

Britain's pre-war fire service was made up of over 1,000 separate brigades, each with its own equipment, methods, and command structures. Greater London alone had 67 different brigades – as the expected prime target for future air raids, this was

NFS light trailer pump crew. Their service badge shows them to be from Fire Force 16, covering Dorset and west Hampshire. The section officer (second from left) is wearing four service chevrons on his right forearm, indicating four years' service. The crew is unusual in that it contains both women and men.

clearly unsatisfactory, and in February 1939 it was decided that, in the event of war, all the Greater London Brigades were to become a single command, under a regional officer. The rest of the country, however, would carry on as before.

The massive fire raids, on London and Coventry among others, starkly displayed the inadequacies of the system. Reinforcements were sent from dozens of different brigades, but on arrival many were unable to help – their hoses had different connections to the local hydrants. Co-operation was made difficult due to confusion caused by different command structures and operating methods.

For these and other reasons, in August 1941 the National Fire Service was created – a single, unified force made up of all the various brigades. This entailed a vast reorganisation: every serving fireman lost his rank, and a board selected officers according to ability. Frank Padgham said: 'During the summer of 1941, the government decided to nationalise the fire brigades, which became the National Fire Service; we were now in a region covering a large part of the south coast. I was promoted to Leading Fireman; I was moved frequently and served in Gosport, Fareham and Aldershot, before returning to Portsmouth prior to the D-Day invasion.'

This immense force, totalling 350,000 at its height at the end of 1942, was largely made up of full-time members split into 39 fire forces, each of which was split into four divisions, consisting of two columns (each totalling 100 pumps), with a reserve of 20 pumps. A company had ten pumps, and a section, five.

Overall, the NFS was commanded from the Home Office fire control room in London. Each CD region had a chief regional fire officer on the staff of the regional commissioner, who acted as liaison between the commissioner and the fire force commanders within his region. Each fire force commander had his own headquarters from where he kept in contact with his divisional HQs and control rooms. There were also mobile control units – specially adapted vans with distinctive red and white chequered markings – which were used at large incidents.

A group of NFS women from Fire Force 6, East Yorkshire. The firewomen are wearing both ski-caps and side-caps, while the two senior officers (front left and centre) are wearing peaked caps.

NFS woman. The picture shows the side-cap in detail; the lighter areas (peak and central insert) are red, service badge and plain buttons in chrome.

Experience taught the necessity for closer co-operation with the CD general services – this was partly brought about by the fact that the NFS controlled the Fire Guard operationally, and also trained with the general services to take their part in the search for anti-personnel bombs. Ultimately, large numbers were trained in light rescue work by Civil Defence instructors.

During lulls between raids, training and drills, NFS personnel worked allot-ments, made or repaired toys for use in nurseries, and did war work such as assembling aircraft wirelesses.

A large number of firemen from other parts of the country were drafted to the south coast in preparation for the Normandy landings, as it was expected that the massive build-up of the armed forces would mean heavy raids. Further, the huge ammunition dumps building up around the area vastly increased the chances of accidental conflagrations.

The NFS had its own mobile reserves, called Flying Columns, which included not only pumps, but staff cars, motorcycles, and even tea cars and a canteen. After D-Day, five such columns were formed to go overseas with the forces; in the end only one went into Europe, working with the US Army.

The Fire Guard

At the beginning of the war, the wardens were the only specific fighters of incendiary bombs. This was not helped by the fact that, until October 1940, they had no legal right of entry to private property. With the dropping of numerous incendiaries, the need for a far larger body of trained personnel was soon recognised.

The Ministry made repeated appeals to householders to form fire parties with their neighbours, and wardens trained them in the proper use of the stirrup pump. But in many areas there were never enough volunteers. In September 1940 the Fire Watchers Order was introduced. This placed a duty on the owners or occupiers of business premises to ensure that, at all times, a person designated as fire watcher was present on the premises. Employees took turns at fire watching – theoretically. In bigger firms, the system tended to work well but in many small concerns it was, at best, erratic.

In October the Access to Property Order conferred powers of entry on wardens and others, but all these measures failed to prevent 'the Second Great Fire of London' in December 1940. On the last day of that year, Herbert Morrison made his famous 'Britain shall not burn' broadcast, and soon after he secured an order giving him the power to register people for fire watching, with the Ministry of Labour directing them to the service. In February, the wardens' service became responsible for recruiting, training and organising fire watchers. At the beginning of August 1941 the existing fire watchers and street parties were re-organised into the kernel of a new, expanded, group – the Fire Guard.

The duty of the Fire Guard was to put out incendiaries and stop fire from spreading, under the direction of their own officers. As soon as it became clear that support was required, a message was sent to their sector point. From there reinforcements would be sent out and the NFS contacted. Once the NFS arrived and commenced operations, all the Fire Guard in the area came under their control.

Compulsory Enrolment Orders were used to recruit the large number of new members required, and one year later a new order introduced a step that even Germany never took – the conscription of women. In January 1942 the links with the wardens' service became even stronger when chief wardens became de facto heads of the local Fire Guard Service; similarly head wardens, head fire guards, and senior wardens, senior fire guards. Alan Barron was a warden in Hurstpierpoint:

Fire guards in fire control room. At least two are wearing firemen's belts and axes, several have City of London helmets and the man fourth from right is wearing a St John first aid badge.

'I had been busy training my Fire Guard groups, making an effort to stage extra stirrup pump practices using large thunderflash fireworks and dustbin lids to teach them how to tackle the new explosive incendiary bombs.'

Local authorities had to devise Fire Guard schemes such as this one by the Leeds wardens' service: the fire guards did duty on rota with a stirrup pump team comprising three members – one to operate the pump, one to use the hose and one to replenish the water. In towns, there would be about seven stirrup pump teams to every 30 houses or, roughly, 150 yards of street. These teams would be under the control of a street party leader, who made up the rota for fire guards, was responsible for the distribution and upkeep of equipment, and organised their training, which included the characteristics of different incendiary bombs, using fire-fighting equipment and appliances, both as individuals and as team members, and methods for giving warnings and passing on information. ARP handbook no. 14, *The Fire Guard's Handbook*, was produced in March 1942 to aid this training. During a raid the street party leader's duties included organising the teams, calling on reinforcements from other neighbouring parties, or alternatively, despatching members to areas needing reinforcement when directed to do so by the street captain and deciding whether to call out off-duty members of the Fire Guard; this was often done by banging on dustbin lids, or by blowing whistles.

Fire Guard street captains were normally in charge of up to six street party leaders and between 50 and 150 fire guards. They organised the Fire Guard in their area, overseeing training and issue of equipment, and made arrangements for reinforcements, including setting up rallying points. During a raid, the street captain was in operational control of the Fire Guard in his area, deciding which parties needed reinforcing and by whom, keeping in contact with the wardens' service and, if required, summoning NFS assistance.

A senior fire guard, working under the local senior air raid warden, was in charge of the street captains in the senior warden's area. They were responsible for the compilation of records of the fire guards in their area, organising training and arranging exercises. During raids, they visited attacked districts, directed street fire party leaders and their parties and, if necessary, took operational control. After the raids they were responsible for preparing and submitting reports to the head fire guard.

The head fire guard was in control of all senior fire guards in a district, and thereby the entire Fire Guard in that district. The head fire guard was responsible for the training of Fire Guard officers; senior fire guards, street captains and leaders, and for keeping them up to date with training methods and information.

Next came the assistant fire guard staff officer, responsible to the divisional warden for the efficiency of the fire guards in their division. The main duty of the assistant Fire Guard staff officer was to oversee the efficiency of Fire Guard officers in the division.

At the head of local Fire Guard organisation was the Fire Guard staff officer. It was his duty to submit incendiary attack and casualty reports to the chief warden, and to make out monthly reports on the efficiency of the fire guards, including numbers available, progress of training, and any assistance received from the

Ellen Wilkinson MP, head of the Fire Guard organisation, inspects Plymouth Fire Guards. Notice the helmet rank markings, and how few of the fire guards possess a uniform.

Home Guard or Army. The Fire Guard staff officer also held weekly meetings of the assistant Fire Guard staff officers, where instructions from the regional HQ or local authority were discussed. Nationally, the MP, Ellen Wilkinson, who had been appointed Under Secretary in charge of Shelters by Herbert Morrison, was made officer commanding the Fire Guard organisation. She worked through the regional organisation via the regional fire guard officer.

Fire Guard depots were set up under depot superintendents from which fire guards could be deployed to reinforce the local area.

Joyce Loysen was conscripted into the Fire Guard in London: 'I did duty in Upper Wimpole Street. I was given a stirrup pump, a helmet and an armband. We were based in the garage of a huge block of flats called Harley House. I did about three nights a week; when there was no raid I used to sleep in the back of a Rolls-Royce or a Daimler, in an imitation fur coat. It was a bit cramped but at least it was warm – the seats were real leather and padded!'

From the end of 1940 the Germans began to use a device aimed directly at those trying to fight the fire bombs, the explosive incendiary. Soon after it had begun to burn – and while it was still possible for an individual to put it out with sand, or a stirrup pump – it would explode, showering anyone trying to put it out with burning magnesium. The *Lewisham Borough News* recorded the death of Roy Crosby, aged sixteen, '. . . who was killed by the explosion of an incendiary bomb which he went to extinguish. Roy recently became a fire watcher. When incendiaries fell near his home he rushed to put one out. His father and sisters, who

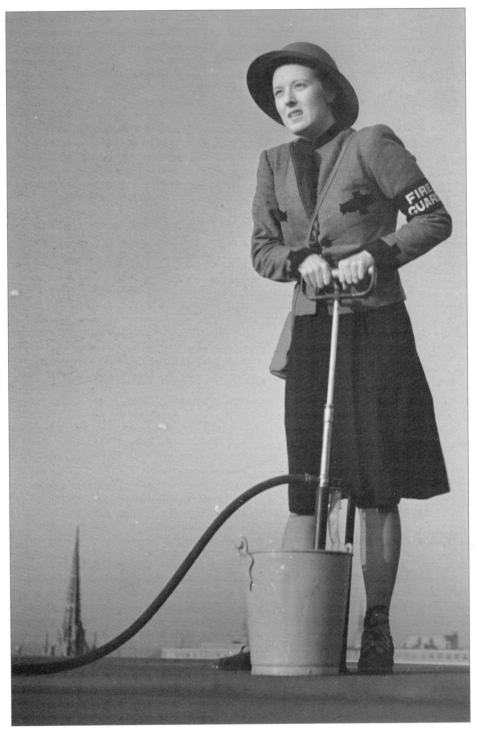

Woman fire guard operating a stirrup pump. (Imperial War Museum)

were in the street, were horrified to see that he was injured. Roy was probably the youngest fire watcher. He was attached to a Catford ARP post. Although he was under age, he was taken on because of his great keenness to do his bit.'

The Baedeker raids of 1942 finally finished off the idea of fire watching. Fire prevention and fire fighting was what was needed. At this point, Fire Guard numbers were at their peak – almost 6 million. In February 1943, the Minister of Home Security announced the introduction, from April, of the Fire Guard Plan, which made the Fire Guard a separate service under the local authority.

Control of the local Fire Guard shifted to the fire guard staff officer, who became the fire guard officer. Head fire guards became area fire guard captains, and senior fire guards, sector captains. The Fire Guard Plan created a system which allowed the greatest co-operation between the Fire Guard and the NFS. The plan divided the country into Fire Guard divisions based on the areas served by NFS stations, with divisions split up into sectors.

In areas where there was a high risk of fire, the Fire Guard was supplied with wheelbarrow pumps,

Fire guard demonstration. The two women on the hose are wearing civilian-style helmets with SFP (street fire party) markings, and early ARP bluette overalls; the Fire Guard Area Officer (the whitehat on the right) is wearing military-style helmet and full CD uniform. This was typical: ordinary fire guards were rarely issued with anything other than helmet and armband, but officers usually had full uniform. (Kent Messenger Group Newspapers)

and teams of three were trained in their use, and in other fire-fighting skills.

At first, NFS instructors trained the fire guards, later, Fire Guard training officers and others involved in training completed week-long courses at the Falfield and Easingwold schools. Those passing would be awarded a 'Fire Guard Instructors Course', or FGIC, certificate, which qualified them to train local instructors at regional or local authority schools. At these schools, 'Instructors FGIC' would conduct slightly shorter courses. Successful candidates would become 'Instructors LFGI' – Local Fire Guard Instructors, who would pass on their knowledge at local depots.

From September 1944 the numbers of fire guards required began falling rapidly. This continued until their disbandment at the end of the war.

CHAPTER 13

Women's Voluntary Service

One of the biggest problems for ARP in the early years was recruitment. It had always been thought that women would make up a fair proportion of the services, especially in report and control, the wardens' and casualty services. There were many reasons for the distinct shortage of women, not least a real reluctance on the part of many local ARP officials to include women. This was not altogether surprising at a time when women were very much seen as weak, unintelligent and helpless. To overcome this, the Home Secretary asked the Marchioness of Reading, Stella Isaacs, to come up with a scheme to encourage women to become involved. This led to the setting up of the Women's Voluntary Service, now the Women's Royal Voluntary Service.

In June 1938 the Women's Voluntary Services for ARP, as it was originally called, was formed. Their first tasks were recruiting and training women for the various ARP services but from the earliest days they displayed a willingness to take on all sorts of jobs which did not fall into the remit of the other services. Early examples included, of course, evacuation, and the lesser-known task of making medical supplies, pyjamas, nursing gowns and bandages.

Barbara Daltrey recalled: 'I remember when war broke out, my mother and I made bandages out of old sheets. I went around the area collecting the sheets from houses – we were quite poor, and sometimes mother said, "these sheets are better than ours, we'll swap them over".' In September 1938, the *Evening Standard* quoted the public relations officer of the WVS: 'Thirty-eight different branches of ARP work are being recruited from makers of surgical dressings (who may be elderly and can work from home), to storekeepers, dispensers, waitresses, time-keepers, clerks, stenographers, and book keepers to state only a few.'

To mark this wider role, in February 1939 their name was changed to the Women's Voluntary Services for Civil Defence, although they were usually just called the WVS. With the coming of the blitz, a great deal of their time was taken up with post-raid work; supplying and running rest centres and mobile canteens, providing hot drinks and snacks to both Civil Defence workers and those bombed out and injured at an incident. A WVS representative was often present at control centres to co-ordinate the despatch of mobile canteens to larger incidents. They also provided shelter marshals who went on duty every time the alert sounded.

This article from the *Lewisham Borough News* gives some idea of the range of activities carried out.

ANNUAL MEETING OF THE FOREST HILL WVS

The valuable work being undertaken by the Central Hospital Supply Service was reviewed by Caroline, Lady Bridgeman, Regional Officer for the London Region CHSS, at the annual meeting of Forest Hill Depot for hospital Supplies, Surgical Dressings and Comforts for the Forces (Women's Voluntary Services), on 23 April.

Lady Bridgeman said the organisation is divided into twelve regions. The duty of the regional officer is to receive material for the manufacture of comforts etc., and to issue this material to work parties in the various districts. . . . There are twelve London clearing houses for dealing with the work . . . to date, a total of 1,134,303 garments have been made by voluntary workers from materials issued by the CHSS. The organisation was constantly receiving gifts from every corner of the world. . . . In return the CHSS sent badges which were proudly worn by donors of innumerable nationalities.

After the last heavy raid, said Lady Bridgeman, the organisation issued 10,000 night-gowns to hospitals. Whatever people might say about night-gowns being out-of-date nightwear, there was no doubt, she commented, that women appreciated them when they were in hospital.

Then there was the library work undertaken by the organisation, the provision of accommodation for 10,000 convalescents, the work of tracing missing and wounded people, and helping people to visit sick relatives. Particularly valuable work was done in caring for lonely old people who felt the strain of war conditions so much more than the young.

WVS salvage workers. The area organiser (centre) is wearing the WVS felt hat and overcoat with cloth service and area badges on her right forearm, and chrome area controller badge on her lapel. The outer two are wearing WVS overalls and berets. (Imperial War Museum)

The Princess Royal in WVS uniform inspects Hull AFS, 1941. Of interest are the officers'
breast badges and the metal epaulettes of the fireman second from right. (Hull Central Library)

WVS housewife.

Another of the big jobs they did was organising salvage. Shortages had led to rationing and the removal of railings from public buildings. Today's recycling schemes pale into insignificance compared with their paper drives, rubber drives, collections of aluminium pots and pans, old bones, rose hips for syrup, old clothes and so on. Other tasks included finding and preparing suitable buildings for war nurseries, then equipping, decorating, and finally staffing them. Another famous scheme in rural areas was the meat pie scheme, under which the WVS daily cooked and delivered pies to thousands of farm workers who would otherwise have received no hot food at lunchtime.

Any mother of a growing child at the time would know how difficult it was to make the clothing ration stretch.

The WVS clothing stores, where people who had been bombed out received new clothes, or mothers could exchange clothes which were now too small, played an important part in civilian life. This was complemented with talks on 'make do and mend' by WVS officials, and the introduction of 'Food Leaders', many of whom were WVS members. Food leaders would give talks on recipes and nutrition using rationed foods, and cooking methods in post-raid conditions, where gas, electricity and other services were interrupted.

Len Wright remembers the WVS:

> I was in a PoW camp near Brunswick, which was relieved by the Americans in April 1945. We were flown to an Oxfordshire aerodrome and handed over to the WVS. By interrogation they learnt our regiments, ranks, and our intended destinations for our PoW entitlement leave of, I think, six weeks, and we were measured. Then we had a very good meal, handed over all our clothing and went to bed in a bed with sheets!
>
> Next morning we were given new underwear, shirts, socks, boots, and battledress bearing our regimental insignia and rank, plus rail warrants and an advance of pay. Fantastic service!

A green and red uniform was designed for WVS workers, although it was never compulsory. There were no ranks as such, only jobs. This meant that a centre organiser, say, could not give orders to other WVS members, except when organising her area.

Rescue men being given tea at the site of an incident. This was one of the many jobs carried out by the WVS housewives' service. (Lewisham Local Studies)

Croydon WVS being inspected by the Duke of Kent. Note the overcoat and suit, and the WVS scarf.

WVS Housewives' Section

Many women were too busy, with young children or other commitments, to give regular time to WVS or CD work, although they were willing to help when they could. For them, the WVS Housewives' Service was formed.

The idea first evolved in Barnes, Greater London, during the latter part of 1938, that women prepared to help would assist their local warden after a raid, looking after elderly people, supplying cups of tea, providing temporary rest for people who had been bombed out and so on. They also assisted in updating the Household Register and fitting gas masks. The scheme worked so well that other local authorities soon began to take it up, and early in 1942 it evolved into the National Housewives' Section of the WVS.

As befits an organisation so closely linked with the wardens' service, the Housewives' Section was organised on similar lines, with the housewives of an area being under the control of a chief housewife, under whom came district leaders, then post leaders and, lastly, street leaders, being equivalent to chief, district, post and sector wardens.

As time went on, many received training in first aid and anti-gas measures; by 1943 it had become common practice for members of the housewives' section to be trained in Fire Guard duties.

Housewives rarely wore uniform, although many wore WVS armbands; instead a special enamelled badge was issued.

CHAPTER 14

Social Activities

Many areas had long periods with no enemy activity and it was at these times that the social side of the services was most important, to hold the teams together and maintain enthusiasm. To this end, social committees were formed and various activities organised.

The wedding of NFS driver Eva Bates to Sergeant Tynan, Royal Marines, 22 May 1943. The carriage is being drawn by marines and NFS women.

One social activity needed no organisation, as the *Lewisham Borough News* of 6 December 1938 reported:

ARP ROMANCES

The co-education system in operation in Lewisham Air Raid Precautions scheme is not only producing efficient volunteers of both sexes but, in two known cases, romances.

After meeting for the first time at a mixed class for the training of prospective wardens, one couple, towards the end of the course, confessed to responsible officials that they had become engaged.

Love at first sight in the other case prevailed at a first-aid class, where a rather younger couple astonished the organisers by the frank declaration that they had decided to become life partners and would be married shortly.

Since quite a rush of volunteers followed the September crisis, it is suspected that there may be other instances of plighted love beside the two mentioned.

As part of Deptford's Warship Week in May 1942, a Brockley Police XI played a Civil Defence XI at the Den. Here, the Civil Defence XI are presented to the Mayor of Deptford before the match. (Lewisham Local Studies)

Children's party in Civil Defence Depot, Hull, December 1943. It was common for posts and depots to host children's parties. (Hull Central Library)

Many local magazines were produced by the different services. *The Collector* was the magazine of the National Fire Service in the west of Scotland, published from May 1940. Its final issue, dated November 1944, covered these social functions: an inter-divisional swimming gala; discussion groups; a divisional billiards league and area snooker and billiards competitions; film shows, including 'the Scottish football team in the USA'; an annual dance; a football team in the Glasgow and District Welfare League; a choir; the NFS pipe band; lectures – including one by 'Mr George Eytle, a resident of British Guyana, . . . [who] gave a most instructive lecture in Birrells Station on "the West Indies"' and, 'at Clydebank, Air Commodore Cockram delivered a pleasant address on "Life in Canada"'. The magazine also reported on a divisional badminton club, a rugby club, a golf tournament, and the 'Firecrackers' concert party.

Another issue from August of that year includes reports on such summer activities as a company sports day, an area tug-of-war final, a proposal for a cricket

The Firecrackers NFS concert party in 1945, including the NiFtieS dance troupe, and Gus Capaldi (professional name Eric Lynn), back row second from right.

club, a divisional bowling competition, a divisional tennis club, a table-tennis tournament and cycling.

Other activities I have come across include a wardens' angling club, a CD swimming gala, a London Fire Force football cup, and a choral society. Lewisham had a Civil Defence Sports Association, where members of the different services competed in leagues and cups. These included police and NFS teams as well as ambulance, control and wardens' teams, and teams from various combined depots. Their annual sports day included a 'white hats race'. Other popular functions included annual wardens' or fire watchers' dances.

Eva Tynan (WAFS) commented:

There was a social side, we had anti-aircraft and searchlight posts down the road, and dances and so on were arranged, there was also a Free French unit. They threw a Christmas party – my officer went but I didn't want to, so I arranged to pick him up later. They had a Christmas tree there – guess what it was hung with – condoms! Several of the girls went – the station officer told me to take them in my car. Well, there was wine there and they all got drunk. I brought them back and they were sick in the back of the car – it was everywhere. So I told the station officer that I'd have to have another car for my officer – he'd told me to take the girls, they'd made the mess, they should clear it up in the morning – I got the new car!

Gus Capaldi was a member of the NFS in Glasgow: 'Late in the war, the [Scottish Brigade's] Western No. 1 area formed a concert party, called the Firecrackers. I was invited to join. I'd been singing for some time – I was in a trio with two other firemen; we were all bald, so we called ourselves 'the Baldwin brothers'. I was principal tenor, singing under the name of Eric Lynn.' Also in the revue were a female dancing troupe, the 'NiFtieS', and the NFS show orchestra: 'We played all over the country, about once a month or so, in cinemas, town halls and so on.'

As the services began to disband in 1945, various wardens' and other Civil Defence associations were formed so that their members could keep in touch.

Fire guards stand by in the shelter of a house porch, stirrup pump ready.

Bibliography

Area Eight, Stroud Defence Committee, 1945
Atlas at War, Atlas, 1945
The Battle of South London, Crystal Publications, 1944
The Changing Face of Britain, Methuen, 1940
Citizens in War – and After, Harrap, 1945
City of Goucester Civil Defence, City of Gloucester, 1946
Civil Defence, HMSO, 1955
Croydon Courageous, Croydon Times, 1946
Croydon and the Second World War, Croydon Corporation, 1949
Dover Front, Secker & Warburg, 1941
Essex at War, Essex County Standard, 1945
Fire Service Memories, Andrew Melrose, 1948
Front Line, HMSO, 1942
Hell's Corner 1940, Kent Messenger, 1942
Home Front Lines, Methuen, 1941
It Came to Our Door, Underhill, 1946
The Lesson of London, Secker & Warburg, 1941
Lloyd's under Fire, Lloyd's, 1947
The Metropolitan Police at War, HMSO, 1947
Ordeal by Fire, Secker & Warburg, 1941
Rescue Service Manual, HMSO, 1942
The Second Great War, Waverley Book Co., 1946
Tactical Training in ARP, S. Evelyn Thomas, 1939
Trial by Ordeal, Malden & Coombe Borough Council, 1946
War on the Line, Southern Rail, 1946
William Carries On, Newnes, 1942

Official Publications

ARP/CD industrial bulletins
ARP handbooks
ARP/CD training bulletins
ARP/CD training manuals
CD training pamphlets
Emergency Medical Services Memoranda
Leeds CD Wardens' Service pamphlet – Fire Guard Organisation, Training and Duties

Newspapers and Periodicals

The Collector – magazine of the NFS Western No.1 Area (Scotland)
Daily Herald Sept 1938
Daily Mirror Oct 1940
Evening News Sept/Oct 1938
Evening Standard 1938 – 1939
Lewisham Borough News 1938 – 1942
The Scout Oct 1939

Index

Place Names Mentioned in the Text